NO CHOICE
NO VOICE
SOMETHING'S ROTTEN
TO THE CORE

Karen Lamoreaux

NO CHOICE,

NO VOICE

SOMETHING'S ROTTEN

TO THE CORE

By

Karen Lamoreaux

www.PaperbackExpert.com

Permission to reproduce or transmit in any form or by any means, electronic or mechanical, including photocopying and recording, or by an information storage and retrieval system, must be obtained by contacting the author through his website.

ISBN-13: 978-1502390660

ISBN-10: 1502390663

Foreword

Very few books have been forged through more grit and tenacity than this powerful expository work. Karen Lamoreaux is a leading force in the grassroots effort that seeks to educate parents on the Common Core State Standards Initiative. While she credits me with introducing her to the issue, I fully credit her with educating me and thousands of others on the miles of political red tape and big corporate sponsorship. We don't need companies like Exxon Mobil paving the way for students to compete in the "global economy." We need teachers who have the freedom to teach in the manner they believe is best for their students. They shouldn't be required to teach standards with an unproven success rate, standards driven by yet another standardized test.

Like most parents, my initial complaint with the CCSSI focused on the bizarre new math methods, which Karen aptly named "caveman math." Shortly after the beginning of the 2013-2014 school year, Karen and I began texting each other pictures of our kids' assignments that contained common core themes. I introduced her to a couple of common core Facebook sites and she soon introduced me to ten more. I recommended a couple of books I had found enlightening on the subject. She quickly informed me that she had already read them, plus a few more. I was on a mission to educate myself in order to successfully supplement my boys' education in areas which were clearly deficient. Karen was on a mission to fight the initiative and get it out of our schools. Nationwide. It was evident that she had taken a leading role in this effort and I was more than happy to become her understudy. My fourth grader likes to boast that Karen used *his* "caveman math homework" as an example during several of her television appearances. She's kind enough to let him believe he ignited a revolution. I'm thrilled we were able to provide a small portion of the ammunition.

I firmly believe this is indeed an education revolution. I've always said I would want Karen Lamoreaux on my side in any fight. This is no exception. She has an indomitable spirit and an amazing ability to persevere in the face of opposition. I had the privilege of attending an Arkansas State Board of Education meeting with her in late 2013. During one of the breaks, a board member approached Karen and employed fake southern charm to try to convince her that her opposition to common core was futile. "It has already been decided. While we value your opinion and will listen to your public comments, the choice to adopt the standards has been finalized. The standards will not be rolled back." With a tone comprised of equal parts sugar and contempt, Karen replied, "One thing you should know about me is that I don't take being told no very well. The quickest way to get something done is to tell me I can't do something." Five hours after the meeting started, Karen got her designated four minutes to speak in front of the board. Within the very same hour, a video of her comments was launched on YouTube and to date it has received over one million views.

The lines were drawn in the sand long before Karen spoke in front of the board. She already knew what she was up against, but I was an understudy and just connecting the dots. Sitting next to her in that moment, I understood the depths of her passion. I realized she was up against an enormous propaganda machine fueled by the federal government. I also knew she wasn't scared. She was energized. Karen Lamoreaux is fighting for the future of our children. She is fighting to ensure that their rights are protected for generations to come. She is fighting to give teachers a voice, when they feel too threatened to speak for themselves. She is fighting to protect the values our founding fathers risked their lives to ensure. She is a modern day patriot. She is my friend and I'm so thankful she's on my side. I wouldn't want her to be anywhere else. After reading her book, you won't either.

—Aimee Galbraith,

Mother of Two and Friend of a Revolutionary

Introduction

"My name is Karen. I'm a mother of three... I am here today not speaking just on behalf of myself. I'm here representing one thousand, one hundred and ten other parents, educators, and tax-payers in our state who have some very serious reservations about the Common Core Initiative."

And at that moment, everything changed. The moment when, unbeknownst to me at the time, I went from being Karen Lamoreaux, mother of three to being Karen Lamoreaux, (accidental) activist mother of three, fighting Common Core and all its baggage. The moment that eventually would lead me to write a book. This book.

My purpose in writing this book is to take a look, from a parent's perspective, at the most recent education reform plaguing our nation, the Common Core State Standards Initiative (CCSSI). It is meant to be a relatively understandable read for the busy "everything to everyone"—the minivan-driving mom, the hardworking dad determined to provide for his family's every need and want, and even the doting grandparent. This is for those of us who have been busy taking care of the everyday things like meals and laundry, driving our kids to rehearsals and practices, coaching games and quietly living, so entrenched in our own day-to-day lives, that much has gone unnoticed. Meanwhile elitists have "slowly boiled" us into education reform that spends our tax money without representation and takes away our parental rights. We're like the frog that didn't jump out of the pot until it was boiled because the rise in temperature was so slow.

This is by no means a comprehensive study of the CCSSI and all its ugly reforms; rather, it seeks to give the reader a brief peer review. I hope it will inspire you to do your own research further into the issue. There's a lot out there—the total research against this reform looks more like a collection of encyclopedias than a paperback.

Catching up on 40 years of corrupt education reform is a great way to pass the time in between loads of laundry or waiting in the carpool line. When the baby is up at 4 a.m. and you know it's too risky to go back to sleep, I hope you'll pick up this book and make that time productive. Then I hope you'll join other parents and take action. The Arkansas Department of Education only gives me three minutes to speak at their meetings. I hope *you* will give me about 200 pages to state my case.

This book combines research from parent-led coalitions around the country, education advocacy groups, my own research and personal journal entries in an honest, sometimes sarcastic style I hope you'll find easy to read. I've tried to provide a spoonful of sugar with the critical information you need to make an informed decision about Common Core, the future of public education and our individual rights as parents and students in a free America.

Table of Contents

Chapter
1

Caveman Math

*"We are not speaking here of arbitrariness in any sense.
Mathematics is not like a game whose tasks are determined by arbitrarily stipulated rules. Rather, it is a conceptual system possessing internal necessity that can only be so
and by no means otherwise."*
~ David Hilbert

HOMEWORK HORRORS

My 4th-grade son arrives home from school. We have a snack and he gets busy doing homework. He has a math worksheet he can't figure out. In an instant, he is crying in frustration, his hands over his face.

"What's the matter? Did you have a bad day today?"

"I can't do this assignment, Mom! I think I need the tiles. The tiles are at school! Ugh!!!" He slides his work across the table in frustration, inches away from panic.

"What tiles? What are you talking about?"

"The tiles! They're in a box at school. We line them up and count them. Or, I could use my hundreds chart. Where's my hundreds chart? Ugh! I can't find it anywhere. I think it's in my desk!" Now he's in full panic mode.

He continues to wail. Now he's pacing and kicking things across the floor.

I have never seen my son behave this way over homework. He's always been a great student and his math scores were in the above-average percentile on those dreaded standardized tests last year. He's never struggled academically. What is going on?

As I examine the assignment, I see it includes word problems calling for simple multiplication, but it asks for drawings to support the answer. Drawings? It looks ridiculous to me. I'm not sure I can figure it out, even with a college education. Have I forgotten elementary math?

I learned my multiplication tables in third grade. My son did not. I assumed he would memorize them this year, but it's well into the first month of his 4th-grade year and we haven't seen any memorization assignments. I don't know how anyone can solve the problems I'm now scrutinizing without knowing the multiplication tables.

I remember, from last year, that awful hundreds chart he's referring to. I hated it. He carried a worn, wrinkled copy of it everywhere so he could complete math problems. We made multiple copies because I would find it shredded and soggy in his pockets when I did laundry, or covered in mysterious sticky goo after he'd left it on the kitchen counter. (Yuck!) I recall feeling irritated that he was being taught to depend on a printed chart instead of doing mental math.

Years from now, when he's an adult making an important financial decision, is he supposed to pull a hundreds chart from his pocket? During homework time, when I tried to get him to do the math in his head, we would tangle over that chart. My daughter, just one year ahead of him, never used a hundreds chart. Like me, she memorized her multiplication tables in third grade. What changed? Is it the teacher? I decide: *I need to schedule a conference with her.*

"Sweetheart, please don't be so upset. I think you're overreacting here. We can do this together. Let's sit down and give it a try."

He is beyond consolation.

My son can't tell me what 4 x 4 equals—or 2 x 3 or any single-digit multiplication answer. He can skip count, though. This means he can count by twos or fives up to the answer. But even then, he has to use his fingers. He should *not* be using his fingers in 4th grade. That works for some problems, but it presents another challenge for him because he has to show his work. This means drawing lots of circles, squares or tally marks to represent his answer. Anything beyond the number five is overwhelming for him.

"I need something to count with! I can't do this Mom! I hate math! I hate it! I'm never going to get it!"

His cries are visceral. But they're coming from the same child who last year said that math was his favorite subject! At the age of ten, he shouldn't need to count "with" anything. He shouldn't panic because he doesn't have something to count *with*.

"Okay, okay calm down, let's find something to use."

I frantically scan the kitchen while he sobs and pounds his fists on the table. I think back to my first grade teacher. She used objects to help us learn math. I remember holding Popsicle sticks and using blocks to learn place value and skip counting. (Later I would learn from some teacher-friends that she used the CGI method, Cognitively Guided Instruction, which uses "manipulatives" such as blocks or tiles, to teach place value in primary grades.) But that was first grade! This is fourth grade. What the heck is going on?

Whatever we chose to count with, there had to be a lot of them, at least 40 or 50. So we choose a box of Kraft Macaroni and Cheese. He uses the raw noodles to perform the math. He keeps losing count of where he left off and having to start over. There is raw macaroni all over the table and on the floor. He keeps running out of room on his paper to draw his many circles, erasing and rewriting in frustration.

When I try to help him, he pushes my hand away in horror and says, "*No*! You're not allowed to write on my paper! It won't count if they know you helped me! Erase that!"

I'm not supposed to help my son with his homework. To make matters worse, this nonsensical assignment, with no instructions or textbook to reference, sends a false message to my son that *I* am math illiterate and unable to assist.

Over two hours later, after drawing over 100 circles and hash marks on his paper, the assignment is done and we are both exhausted and defeated.

∼∽∼∽∼∽∼∽∼∽

In the weeks that follow, he brings home more strange math assignments that create a divide between us and make homework time miserable. No fourth-grader should spend that much time on math homework after a long day.

I see him complete one assignment after another that looks more like art than math. My son has to draw hundreds of circles and hash marks on his paper to find an answer I learned to compute in two simple steps. Each assignment is filled with hash marks and shapes, making his work look like caveman drawings on stone. He cries and has tantrums in frustration. I find myself teaching him "the way I learned it" because the method he's learning in school doesn't make sense to either of us and, quite honestly, won't work in the real world.

CENSORED TEACHERS

I make that appointment for a parent-teacher conference. My conversation with her reveals that my son's homework materials and the teaching methods being used are a result of the Common Core State Standards Initiative (CCSSI) implemented for grades 3-8 in 2012.

She tells me she didn't choose the topics, the materials or the math methods. They were all provided to her. I express my disdain for what I am seeing and experiencing at home, including my concern that my son is not memorizing the multiplication tables yet. I tell her my son can't go through his adult life drawing little circles on paper like a caveman.

I recall a PTO meeting held two years previously, filled with sunshine and applesauce about a new set of standards that we were supposedly working with other states to develop. They were going to prepare our kids for college and we should expect some disruptions in the transition. There was no mention of what we are experiencing now.

The teacher speaks softly. She explains she has no choice but to teach these methods. She tells me that my son isn't the only child who didn't memorize multiplication tables last year. This will present a problem when the class moves to fractions in a few weeks. She plans to do her best to help those children catch up with flashcards and weekly quizzes before then. But she is swamped and overscheduled, struggling to keep up. She cannot stop and make sure all the kids are at the same level. She has to move forward whether the kids grasp the information or not.

I trust her completely and believe she is sincere and doing her best. After all, she is a successful, veteran teacher with an excellent reputation. It seems I will have to help my son learn the multiplication tables myself, if he is to learn them at all—in his spare time, when he's not panicking about his caveman math. I am alarmed at the thought that other children, in the hands of less competent teachers, may be in more trouble than my son is.

Right after this meeting, I visit another educator with over thirty years of experience. I asked her opinion of Common Core. She rises from her desk, closes the door and lowers her voice. I feel like I'm in a spy novel.

She tells me:

She dislikes the Common Core, but gets pushback from administrators when she vocalizes her opinion. Teachers have little or no control over Common Core or over what they teach. If I want it to go away, I will have to work with other parents to make that happen, because teachers have no voice. She is so upset by what she is experiencing that she has seriously considered early retirement.

It is difficult to find veteran teachers with multidisciplinary experience who approve of this reform. The few teachers that seem to like it have a few things in common. Most of them are very new to the profession and very young. They usually teach only one subject and know little about Common Core beyond its impact on their own classroom. Their support generally seems to come in the form of scripted messages from the Common Core State Standards Web Site.

The frustrating part is that many of the veteran teachers and administrators see this as the latest fad program that will come and go just as fast as it arrived. These poor teachers have been bombarded with experiment after experiment, so many constant interruptions to their craft, that they have become jaded.

My further conversations with teachers and parents produce similar responses. Teachers closing doors, speaking in whispers, looking around to see if anyone else is listening before they discreetly express their dissatisfaction with this new reform. Many report to me that they have been threatened with insubordination for speaking against it in meetings. Their emails and social media are now monitored for mutiny. They say one thing at work but when they are "off the clock" and in a setting they consider safe, they share their true feelings about it. The teachers who oppose it insist on communicating with me using separate, personal email addresses instead of their "work" addresses. They are terrified of speaking out publicly and don't discuss this subject on social media sites. They are afraid of the "Bully Bandwagon of Educrats," those education administrators and all of the other meddlers who have jumped on the Common Core bandwagon, using their money, power and influence to bully parents, teachers and local administrators.

THE BULLY BANDWAGON OF EDUCRATS (BBE)

The Bully Bandwagon of Educrats is the corrupt ruling class of the education system: the bureaucrats appointed into powerful positions, with terms lasting longer than our legislators are in office, making change nearly impossible. It includes the superintendents, commissioners and administrators who set our education system's culture just as a CEO sets the culture of a business. Speaking of business, the membership of the BBE also now includes CEOs of multinational corporations. More on that later.

These bureaucrats use bullying tactics and cite policies and proce-dures to tell parents and teachers to shut up and get in line because they are the *State* and they know better. One of them even boasted to me that we, as parents, only "thought" we had local control until this reform came along.

In January of 2014, a superintendent in Petal, Mississippi, John Bu-chanan, threatened his teachers with their livelihood over Common Core. In a public district meeting, he made it clear that teachers who did not favor Common Core should see him so he could help them find a job elsewhere. His teachers were then put on the spot publicly and asked if they supported Common Core. Buchanan, of course, denies that he threatened anyone's job, but says, "In this case, the message was 'If you're not happy teaching Common Core State Standards, see me. Let me know. We'll try to find a place in Mississippi that is not teaching those standards.'" [1]

WHAT IS THIS COMMON CORE?

I am stunned when I hear about this and suddenly feel a strong urge to learn more about Common Core. I pored over hundreds of hours of research into the topic and what I learned was heartbreaking. This was not just a set of standards, as is so frequently claimed. Rather, the Common Core State Standards Initiative is indeed that—an initiative—not just standards. The standards anchor a comprehensive reform initiative with intentions that do not sit well with me. This reform seeks to lead our country toward a managed economy with workforce steering using data mining with public/private relationships and a United Nations (UN)-based model of education.

I find myself awake for long stretches of time in the wee hours of the night, researching, trying to get my head around what I am finding. I learn that our teachers have no voice in their own profession. How sad, how disheartening, how frustrating that must be. And how unfortunate for our children.

Chapter
2

What You Really Need is a Viral Video!

"Our deepest fear is not that we are inadequate,
our deepest fear is that we are powerful beyond measure.
It's our light, not our darkness that most frightens us.
As we liberate from our own fear,
our presence automatically liberates others."
~ Marianne Williamson

WHO'S IN CHARGE HERE?

I don't have a locally elected school board in my own district. The state took over our district due to financial troubles about five years ago. There are no plans on the part of the Bully Bandwagon of Educrats (BBE) to provide parents with elected representation (in the form of a new local school board) any time soon. My only option, to express my concerns, was to go to the State School Board.

Previously, I had no idea this board existed. I learned the State School Board is appointed by the Governor and is comprised of individuals selected to do the Governor's bidding. The same goes for our state education commissioner—appointed, not elected. They are nothing more than an extension of the state. They are not an elected body and therefore not likely to care much about what I, as a voter, have to say. Further, each member serves a seven-year term, almost four times as long as a state legislator serves. I was stunned.

Thanks to some legislation that was passed in the 1990s (which I will address later), the focus of education officially shifted to workforce (labor market) development. Workforce boards and councils were formed to make education policy. The U.S. Chamber of Commerce made it a priority to be part of education reform by infiltrating boards and lobbying legislators for their workforce needs. Now, many local boards that once upon a time may have included one or two members of the commerce community (business owners), are dominated by them, leaving parents and teachers a minority in the representation. As such, appointees to this board are not required to be parents or teachers or to have any experience in the field of education.

When I discuss my concerns with legislators, one common issue that arises is the balance of power with bureaucrats in the state's Department of Education. The legislators, regardless of the preferences of the elected majority, are at the mercy of these appointees with their longer terms. These administrators are often quoted as telling representatives and senators that they will simply "wait them out."

The following information is from the Arkansas State Board of Education web site. It says the Arkansas State School Board, established in

1999, is made up of two members from each of the state's four congressional districts and one member selected at-large. Members are appointed by the Governor for seven-year terms. Further, it says the board is composed of business and community leaders and represents the "diverse population of Arkansas." It notes that the Board meets on the second Thursday and Friday of each month. Their mission statement reads, *"The Arkansas Department of Education strives to ensure that all children in the state have access to a quality education by providing educators, administrators and staff with leadership, resources and training."* [2]

The assertion that this board represents the diverse population of Arkansas is pure propaganda. Just because we have multiple colors and both genders on the board does not mean it matches the diverse population of the state. Notice the board is made up of business and community leaders, not teachers or parents. This confirms that the influence on our education decisions is purely centered on economic and social change. These non-educators are here to provide educators with leadership, resources and training. Seems to me that educators should be leading other educators.

I am not surprised that our teachers are jaded. For many years, their efforts have been directed by people who are clueless about how kids learn or about what goes on in a K-12 classroom. The board seems to view teachers as corporate serfs, not assets or professional peers.

In Arkansas, our State School Board meets during the day and the meetings run for hours. (They sometimes meet on Sunday afternoons, but these meetings are not publicly announced.) Most working parents cannot take time off work every month to attend their meetings, typically scheduled from 9:00 a.m. to 1:00 p.m., two days in a row. Even if they attend, they're only allowed 3 minutes to air their concerns before a board that doesn't seem interested.

The board *does* live stream their meetings on the Internet, providing a false sense of transparency. We can watch, but we really have no power to change their decisions or their decision-making process. The decisions that directly affect my child in public school are made by a group of people who, for the most part, have never taught in a K-12 classroom.

In 2009 the State School Board was given an insurmountable amount of authority by the Arkansas state legislature regarding standards and curriculum, seemingly just in time for the adoption of Common Core. The legislature handed over my education rights to this appointed board of people who are not educators, at the same time silencing my voice as a parent and taxpayer. This was a trend in several others states as well, laying the groundwork for what they refer to and intend to be "sustainable" reform.

By the time I learned all this, I had found the support of a few people at *Arkansas Against Common Core*. We emailed our concerns to the Governor and the Chair of the State Board of Education. It was obvious that the Governor wasn't receiving our emails (or, at any rate, he wasn't *reading* or personally responding to them) and everyone was getting the same response from the Chief of Staff, regardless of the specific concerns raised. For example, I could email a question about privacy concerns and get CCSSI web site propaganda that had nothing to do with privacy.

The responses were extremely condescending and intimidating. Not only that, but most of the responses consisted of "cut and paste" propaganda lifted from CCSSI materials. They all sounded the same: "Thank you for your interest in Arkansas education. Please *allow me to share some information about the Common Core* State Standards Initiative with you..." (Emphasis mine. You'll see why. This BBE mantra quickly acquires the effect of fingernails on a blackboard for anyone opposed to the Common Core.)

SAYING MY PIECE

Finally, I asked to be placed on the agenda for public comment because I wanted my testimony to be shared with the entire board and placed on public record. Permission was granted and I was allotted five minutes to present my concerns.

Wow! How nice of them to allow this parent and taxpayer five *whole* minutes to share my concerns! What a benevolent dictatorship!

The Big Day

I arrive at the meeting site. There are big bright pictures of smiling young children on the old wood-paneled walls. It is a paradox given the tone in the room. The agenda is filled mostly with charter schools begging for permission to operate or to increase enrollment caps. An attorney for the department has to keep reminding the chair that she is obligated to hear public comment after she makes multiple attempts to derail it.

The Assistant Commissioner from the Department of Education gives a brief update on how the Common Core implementation is going. She tells the board that "great things are happening in the classrooms" and that scores are already going up.

This is despite the fact that the documentation in her handout indicated the exact opposite—scores had flat-lined or declined since implementation. I cannot believe that not a single person in the room is questioning this contradiction! Is anyone reading this handout? No. Everyone in the room is looking at their phones instead, probably waiting for their own five minutes. The board watches the Assistant Commissioner, smiling, eyebrows raised like kids in a candy store, hanging on her every cognitively dissonant word.

Another 2 ½ hours go by. (The entire meeting is five hours long and, quite frankly, comes across as a dog and pony show, wasting tax dollars by the minute.) I listen to our State Board's Chair publicly mocking parents who have emailed their concerns about the Common Core to her. Her mockery is echoed by the Assistant Commissioner of the Department of Education. Shaking their heads and rolling their eyes, they accuse us of not being open to change. They call us misinformed conspiracy theorists, hysterics who believe anything we read on the Internet. They laugh at our attempts to voice our concerns. I feel I've been transported back to junior high.

The chair calls for a 30-minute lunch break. She approaches me and asks if I'm the one who sent her the many emails complaining about the Common Core. I answer that I am indeed the author of those emails and I'm looking forward to sharing my concerns with the rest of the board. (*Am I ever.*)

Then, in a condescending tone, she tries to talk me into leaving, saying it will be a very long meeting and maybe I should just go home and come back another day. She even shakes her finger at me when she speaks. *Not* the way to get on my good side.

WHAT YOU REALLY NEED IS A VIRAL VIDEO

I stand up and tell her I have taken an entire day off work to be at this meeting and I will make my voice heard. If I have to wait, that's fine. She makes a point of telling me she used to be a senator and says my efforts are in vain—they're not rolling back the standards. If I wish to see the Common Core rolled back, I will have to do it through the legislature and since they don't meet again for two years, I'm out of luck.

I respond that the quickest way to get something done is to tell me I can't do it. My blood is boiling. I feel my friend gently place her hand on my arm and it centers me. I smile at this bully and say I will wait and deliver my remarks as planned.

Inner rant that followed:

Just who *do our children belong to? Their parents or the State? How is it that parents are being told to step aside while the state has its way? Education is a taxpayer service. These people work for us. We pay their salary.*

A little more coherently: *Under the current arrangement, public discourse regarding education decisions is effectively shut down and parents are reduced to a ceremonial five-minute opportunity to voice their concern, which clearly falls on deaf ears. Under this arrangement, I have no voice!*

Back to the dog and pony show...

By the end of this five-hour meeting and public mocking, I was furious. At lunch, the chair told me that even though their email promised me five minutes to speak, now I would only have three. I have to whittle some things down.

I frantically make last minute changes to the testimony I had painstakingly prepared for more than two weeks. When they call my name, I give my fiery testimony to the State Board. I'm so angry my voice trembles.

AN ACCIDENTAL ACTIVIST

Unbeknownst to me, my speech was streamed live on the Internet. A friend recorded it and placed it on YouTube. Before I could blink, my testimony hit home with so many other parents, it went viral. In just 24 hours, it had 30,000 views. Suddenly I was flooded with letters from parents and teachers all over the country, all of them supportive. I began hearing from other parents who didn't like caveman math.

The censorship of our teachers here in Arkansas was obvious. Many Arkansas teachers felt the same way. Afraid of losing their jobs, none commented publicly. But I received many comments "under the radar." Below are just two examples of letters from local teachers after the video went viral:

- "I can't post anything publicly or even join the program for fear of losing my job. But I do want to thank you for standing up and speaking out on this. I know I agree with you because I experience it first-hand. But because of fear of losing my job, I have not been able to stand up and voice my concerns. They won't. I've tried. Teachers are scared to go against them. All I know is teaching. I've been doing it 15 years so the idea of losing my job is tragic for me. A lot of teachers have left public education and gone to private schools instead of fighting against the system. It's a fight we feel we can't win. Our jobs are threatened almost daily. We are too scared to fight. Please feel free to inbox me if you have any questions or concerns."

- "I'm scared. I'm scared mostly because we have a group of kids who are being the guinea pigs... mine among them...They (teachers) are overwhelmed, stressed and apprehensive. Kids feel the stress... Please keep my comments to you anonymous. Most teachers (that I have contact with daily) hate CC because they feel... that we are going to be asking kids to do things they can't do. In addition, most fear speaking out."

Parents have no choice, no voice. We can't run for these appointed positions and our brief appearances before the board seem pointless. Teachers have no choice but to carry out the will of this board. Parents have been pushed aside in favor of those with money and political influence. After all, they know better, right?

A VOICE IN OUR SOCIETY

Six months later, our little group, *Arkansas Against Common Core*, founded by Grace Lewis, had tripled in membership and elected an organized board. As I write this only six months later, the video has had almost 1,000,000 views and has rallied over 8,000 parents in Arkansas against the Common Core.

Turns out if you want a voice in our society these days, what you need is a viral video. I was terrified when the video was placed on YouTube and started to go viral. I wasn't prepared to be the face of the opposition to Common Core in Arkansas.

I knew nothing about politics, was not an activist and clearly I had no previous knowledge about education policy. I truly had no idea of how the education system worked or how things really took place at my state capitol before I started this journey. In fact, I had never set foot in my state capitol except to look at the Christmas tree and lights in December!

I had become an accidental activist, committing myself to advocating for my children's privacy, our educational rights and most of all, for freedom. I discovered I am not alone—and neither are you.

Chapter

3

The Buzzing of the Corporate Worker Bees

"If ye love wealth better than liberty, the tranquility of servitude than the animating contest of freedom, go from us in peace. We ask not your counsels or arms. Crouch down and lick the hands which feed you. May your chains sit lightly upon you, and may posterity forget that ye were our countrymen."
~ Samuel Adams

TEACHING OR TRAINING?

Since the late 1980s, there has been a paradigm shift in education. We are moving away from a goal of K-12 education developing intellectual, freethinking, innovative individuals with a lifelong love of learning. Instead, like frogs boiling, we have been incrementally moving toward an industrial workforce model of education.

The CCSS Initiative is very much corporate-led versus state-led. It gets funding from the U.S. Department of Labor, particularly for data collection, and has the enthusiastic and tireless support of the U.S. Chamber of Commerce (the largest, most powerful political lobby in America). This makes education policy about economics and power, ultimately leading to a managed economy, not a free market capitalist enterprise. We are losing the emphasis on a well-rounded education that includes an emphasis on literature and individualism in the name of K-12 workforce preparation.

We are training, not teaching.

Parents notice that the people behind CCSSI make up the same small group of elitist individuals and organizations that have been trying to federalize and centralize education in America for generations. Most have no background in teaching, though some have a degree in education. Those without teaching backgrounds have no K-12 classroom insight, while those with education degrees have no interdisciplinary insight. Yet they stand to make a significant profit from experimenting with our children's education.

MARC TUCKER

Marc Tucker is the president of the National Center for Education and the Economy (NCEE) and has been since 1988. His influence is startling considering that he did not major in education, nor has he ever taught in a K-12 classroom. He majored in philosophy and American Literature and mastered in Telecommunications. Together with Lauren Resnick, Mario Cuomo (yes *that* Mario Cuomo, Governor of New York), Hillary Clinton and Ira Magaziner, he has been pushing for *national standards* with America's Choice since 1988.

In 1992, Tucker sent a letter to Hillary Clinton outlining his plan, his vision for education in America. In his "Dear Hillary" letter, he recommends something like the German model of education. He lays out a plan that is coordinated by labor market boards at the local and federal levels, "to coordinate the systems for job training, postsecondary professional and technical education, adult basic education, job matching and counseling" [3]

President Clinton used this letter as a model for his administration's K-12 education reform (seems every president has one these days). In a speech promoting his new reform he touts, "We can no longer hide behind our love of local control of the schools. " [4]Three significant laws were passed that set the stage for the Common Core State Standards Initiative:

- The School to Work Act
- The Goals 2000 Act
- 5th Reauthorization of Elementary and Secondary Education Act (ESEA)

Most parents were unaware of the giant cultural shift in education resulting from these acts. By placing education policy decisions in the hands of the labor market (as advised by Tucker), we shifted K-12 education from an intellectual purpose to an economical one.

Once those laws were passed, the reformers got to work building the State Longitudinal Data Systems (SLDS.) This is a tool for the would-be utopian-managed economy born through a generation of industrial education, with millions of dollars in support from the U.S. Department of Labor - a dream come true for Tucker and a gold mine for private corporations.

School Board Control

Local school boards became top-heavy with greedy labor market merchants and those seeking political gain. These individuals have more money and influence and a better chance at winning elected positions than the average parent—and they do win. Most of them are CEOs and social change agents, who know nothing about early childhood education and have never taught in a K-12 classroom in their lives. The local elected school boards are now dominated by the Chamber of Commerce, three million businesses strong, to influence education based on workforce needs.

Over the years, these local school boards have earned a reputation of corruption and financial mismanagement, leading to school closures and consolidation. Now the national charter movement and the U.S. Department of Education (DOE) wish to eliminate local school boards and make 90% of the public school system chartered. They point the finger of blame at local school boards to justify their corporate takeover of the entire system. What did we expect when we allowed parents and teachers to take a back seat on these local boards in favor of those who define success as profit and political gain? The existence of locally elected school boards is not the problem. Rather, the composition of these boards, coupled with consolidation laws, is the problem.

Contributing to this reinvention of representation is the change in the fabric of family and our view of politics. As our society evolves, more families become dependent on two incomes and overscheduled with multiple activities. They, therefore, become too busy to take on civic responsibilities such as school board positions or even PTO membership.

We are "too busy" to attend school board meetings and hold the board accountable.

We don't like politics. We don't have time. We justify our absence by arguing that "they" are going to do what they want to anyway. That was my attitude. Later, the proponents of Common Core, instead of addressing our concerns sincerely, would try to silence parents by making statements like, "Where were you four years ago?"

The answer is that we were apathetic, ignorant about what was going on and we trusted them. We trusted them with our children. We trusted them with our money. And we got the education system we deserve.

The establishment of appointed labor market state school boards was the nail in the coffin of local control and protection from federal control in our schools. These high profile positions establish a monarchical rule making parents minions of the state. Many parents have no idea these boards even exist, much less how much authority they hold, until something goes gravely wrong. I didn't.

In addition to shifting our representation and effectively removing the voices of parents and teachers, these laws ushered in *labor market information systems*," also known as State Longitidunal Data Systems (SLDS). Additionally, they increased federal involvement with a push for (dreaded) national standards and tests.

Based on the German system, Tucker's approach to education is economic, designed to *train* for jobs and meet global workforce needs, instead of intellectual, providing a well-rounded education. According to Joy Pullman of The Heartland Institute, "Tucker advocated implementing national standards, created by a board that forms the standards based on skills needed for particular jobs. Children would receive admittance into postsecondary education if they met the criteria and developed the skills *dictated by the standards*. Labor market boards would post all jobs, public and private, that the students with specific skill sets could earn. In Tucker's system, the purpose of individuals is to serve the economy, and the economy does not exist to serve the individual. The purpose of this type of education is to create workers to drive the economy instead of to create free citizens. This shift is manifested in the Common Core, which follows the system Tucker supports."[5] (Emphasis mine.)

Thanks to the policies of the 1990s and Tucker's influence on K-12 education, we now have an entire generation of education policy-makers and legislators who think this is how it has always been and should be. Many reformers truly believe that K-12 education should be geared at managing the economy and they use economic statistics to scare parents into agreeing with this philosophy.

PLAYERS AND PAYERS

The education and workforce program of the U.S. Chamber of Commerce, known as the Institute for a Competitive Workforce, received a total of 4.6 million dollars from The Bill and Melinda Gates Foundation between 2009 and 2012 under the "global policy and advocacy," "Postsecondary Success" and the "College-Ready U.S. Program" categories.

Like the powerful U.S. Chamber of Commerce, the Business Roundtable, with over 200 member corporations, is pushing for Common Core in the name of their workforce. In September of 2013, President Obama rounded them up in a conference and asked the CEOs to step up to the propaganda campaign and consider using their own marketing dollars to do so. Exxon Mobile was one of the first to step up with commercials, along with Intel™ and Cisco™ Systems.

Intel™ is promoting Common Core with its employees and asking them to support it publicly at community events. By their own admission, Intel™ says that about half of their employees do not know what Common Core is and many oppose it. One morning I happened to catch Squawk Box on television and, behold! The former CEO of Intel™ and member of the Business Roundtable, Craig Barrett, was spreading propaganda about Common Core and recruiting corporate serfs. (He also owns a charter school and Intel™ provides teacher curriculum resources, so he has an opportunity to make money from the Common Core initiative.) I was struck that Common Core was being discussed on a stock market trading show. He said Common Core is going to "be tough for kids" implying that the Common Core opposition simply isn't willing to push our kids.[6]

Exxon CEO Rex Tillerson jumped on the Bully Bandwagon of Educrats when he threatened a Pennsylvania Governor with his economic power. When Governor Tom Corbett ordered a delay in Common Core implementation, he received this threat from Tillerson, using Pennsylvania students as pawns for economic gain:

> However, I was disappointed to learn of the misinformation opponents of this critical effort are advancing, which subsequently led your administration to delay its implementation. I urge you to make the necessary clarifications quickly and move forward with the Pennsylvania Common Core.

Exxon Mobil has significant operations in Pennsylvania, and we are committed to enhancing the quality of life for all your citizens. Last year, we contributed $3.3 million to Pennsylvania universities, hospitals, environmental research efforts and arts and civic organizations, but I believe there is nothing more important than improving the quality of education. The Pennsylvania Common Core will go a long way to achieving that goal, and it gives Exxon Mobil the confidence that the educational standards we require for employment will be met by your state's graduates.[7]

Threatening letters like this from ego-inflamed corporate CEOs reflect the current state of plutocracy (government by the wealthy) in America. Does power lie with the people or with a few powerful, rich corporations? Have we lost democracy in education?

The Common Core Initiative is the fulfillment of Tucker's dream:

- A dream where education decisions are made by labor market boards claiming the most knowledge of that elusive "21st Century Global Economy."
- A dream with a preschool-to-age-20 data collection initiative with workforce planning and common standards and
- A dream embodied in a system (standards and tests) that is the same for everyone.

This mentality has created politically driven school boards, education policy that results in corruption, increased bureaucracy and loss of local control for parents and teachers. While that culture change was brewing, America slipped into a recession—the perfect "crisis" needed to entice states with federal dollars used as bait to lure them into *sustainable reform*.

Chapter

4

Corporate-Led Education

*"An oligarchy of private capital cannot be effectively checked
even by a democratically organized political society
because under existing conditions, private capitalists inevitably control,
directly or indirectly, the main sources of information."*
~ *Albert Einstein*

ORIGINS MATTER

Many proponents of Common Core argue that it shouldn't matter where reform comes from or who pays for it, as long as it is "good." Marketing techniques that label it "rigorous," "college-ready," "higher order thinking" and so on, would make any parent believe it must be great for their children. And surely, the people working in education are all "good" people, or they appear to be, especially in our 30-second sound-bite society.

The truth is that the ideologies, philosophies and goals of those who bring the Common Core to our classrooms should not be ignored. The individuals, organizations and ideologies *matter* because they will directly influence the next generation. Those individuals writing the standards, the tests and the books and training the teachers must inevitably bring their biases and prejudices with them. Consequently, they will groom an entire generation of voters—I mean, children.

Who are they? How do they envision public education, and do they value public education at all? Or are they in this for other reasons? As fellow *Arkansas Against Common Core* board member Denna Slade asks, "Where are they taking us?"

Let's face it—no government-sponsored program ever gets smaller. Pay no attention, nothing to see here! Just rigorous standards! In the case of education, the federal government has only been expanding its role, most recently with No Child Left Behind (NCLB). We all know how well that worked out. The NCLB outcome based education reform resulted in the closing of valuable neighborhood schools and a mega-testing culture in our classrooms. It was such a failure, that now a waiver from the worst provisions of it is used as an incentive to adopt Common Core!

As a parent, I am a natural interrogator. For instance, before I allow my daughter to spend the night at someone's house, I want to be sure I have a good sense of what the family is like. I want to know that the house is safe. I want to know the parents' child-rearing philosophy is similar to mine. I want to know the intent of the occasion. I'm not content, and she's not going anywhere, until I get satisfactory answers to all my questions.

The classroom is no different. As parents, most of us want to know at least a little about the teacher. We want to know what materials are used for instruction and where they originated. We want to know the educational philosophy of the school.

I set out to determine who was behind Common Core: who wrote it, who is paying for it and the ideologies and philosophies of those individuals and organizations. After all, they will influence my children for at least six hours a day.

This reform is not about education at all. It is about centralized planning, leading to power and profit. This is just a start. If you want a comprehensive look at the reformers, read *A Chronicle of Echoes: Who's Who in the Implosion of American Public Education,* by Mercedes Schneider.

Education in America is a trillion dollar goldmine for profit and ripe for social change. Let's look at the miners...

- NGA – National Governors Association
- CCSSO – Council of Chief State School Officers
- Achieve - David Coleman
- College Board, David Coleman, again
- Pearson Education Foundation
- Bill and Melinda Gates Foundation
- Jeb Bush – Foundation for Excellence in Education

NGA AND CSSO

Let's start with the biggest movers and shakers behind the Common Core, all three based in Washington, D.C. Big surprise there! The National Governor's Association (NGA) and the Council of Chief State School Officers (CCSSO) worked with Achieve, Inc. to draft the standards. This public-private partnership uses taxpayer dollars and minimizes the government's accountability. How convenient!

In 2008, probably before his moving boxes were unpacked in the White House, newly elected President Obama received *Benchmarking for Success* from the NGA, CCSSO and Achieve. It outlined 1) the adoption of a common set of internationally benchmarked standards and 2) assured the alignment of state textbooks, curricula and assessments to these standards as two of the top five priorities.

So who are *these* people? The NGA is a D.C.-based lobby group that serves as a vehicle for developing national policies. Their mission statement reads, "The National Governors Association (NGA) is the bipartisan organization of the nation's governors. Through NGA, governors share best practices, speak with a collective voice on national policy and develop innovative solutions that improve state government and support the principles of federalism."[8] Over half of the operating expenses of this group are paid for with federal tax dollars. [9]

Similarly, the CCSSO is a D.C.-based group for the state school officers. States pay $16,000 per year to be a member of this organization, which holds around 100 meetings annually. About half of the CCSSO operating funds are paid with federal tax dollars. Regarding the CCSSO and Common Core, Joy Pullman of the Heartland Institute says:

> Multiply just one membership fee by 46 participating states
> for a minimum of *$736,000 in tax dollars* the CCSSO receives
> each year for an initiative reshaping nearly every textbook, re-

placing nearly all state tests, overhauling teacher training nationwide, providing the basis to measure teachers, and creating nationwide data repositories for student grades, behavior, attendance, and more.[10]

The CCSSO's mission includes advancing the "continued disaggregation" of student data by sponsoring the Common Education Data Standards (CEDS) Initiative. For the purpose of education reform, they have partnered with Microsoft™, The American Institutes of Research (AIR), McGraw Hill, Pearson Education, Amplify, Scholastic and ACT, just to name a few.[11]

The federal contributions to the CCSSO went up in 2010 when the standards were adopted, as the U.S. DOE gave the NGA and the CCSSO *$330 million* in federal taxpayer stimulus money. The federal government also funds the new assessments—more on *that* later.

Our federal tax dollars fund the very groups that wrote and own the copyright to the Common Core. To say that there is no federal involvement in Common Core is blatantly false.

ACHIEVE & STUDENT ACHIEVEMENT PARTNERS

Achieve (www.achievethecore.org), led by David Coleman, was hired by the NGA and CCSSO to assist in the drafting of the standards. David Coleman was the President of Achieve when the standards were developed. Along with Jason Zimba and Susan Pimentel (all three of whom also worked for him at Achieve Inc.), he also founded a non-profit called Student Achievement Partners. Let's take a look at these three individuals who lead the development of the standards.

Like many others advocating for Common Core, Mr. Coleman is a smart guy, a Rhodes scholar, but not an educator and he has never taught in a classroom in his life. He took a job working for McKinsey on big data instead. He founded the Grow Network, a big data company that analyzes assessment data, and sold it to McGraw Hill.

Coleman admits the group was, "composed of that collection of unqualified people who were involved in developing the common standards." He was also the lead author of the English Language Arts (ELA) standards despite the fact that he admits, "I probably spend a little more time on literacy because as weak as my qualifications are there, in math they're even more desperate in their lacking."[12]

He speaks of having to "convince" governors to adopt these standards, and denounces the use of narrative writing in K-12 education saying:

> Do you know the two most popular forms of writing in the American high school today? ...It is either the exposition of a personal opinion or the presentation of a personal matter. The only problem, forgive me for saying this so bluntly, the only problem with these two forms of writing is as you grow up in this world you realize people don't really give a **** about what you feel or think. What they instead care about is can you make an argument with evidence, is there something verifiable behind what you're saying or what you think or feel that you can demonstrate to me. It is a rare working environment that someone says, "Johnson, I need a market analysis by Friday but before that I need a compelling account of your childhood."[13]

Jason Zimba was the lead math author for Achieve. He holds a Ph.D. in mathematical physics and he, at least, has taught in a classroom at the college level and a few high school courses for struggling students. Sadly, Zimba has no K-12 teaching experience. He was a founding member of Student Achievement Partners, along with David Coleman.

Susan Pimentel co-authored the literacy standards for Achieve. While she holds an education degree, she has never taught in a classroom, instead going on to a law degree. Her private organization was paid millions in "consulting" fees for her contribution to the standards. She also has an organization called "Standards Work!" and sits on the National Assessment Governing Board (NAGB) of mega-testing.

Much like these three individuals leading the charge, most of the "Experts" on the Achieve team are business people from education companies, especially the testing market. The team that developed the standards did not include any K-12 classroom teachers.

How did three people get the funding to create national standards? To date, Achieve Inc. has received $2 million from the Carnegie Foundation, $7 million from GE and millions more from Nationwide, Lumina and State Farm. Achieve also received $23.5 million from the Bill and Melinda Gates Foundation before 2009, with another $13.2 million after the standards were created. The Student Achievement Partners startup was also given $6.5 million from Bill and Melinda Gates.

Further, upon visiting the Achieve web site and reading their Common Core propaganda, one finds that they refer to this initiative as an "agenda," (a word typically used in political arenas) and it goes on to emphasize the importance of student data collection using the P-20 model (Preschool through age 20 tracking). This is despite the fact that most local proponents of Common Core deny that data collection has anything to do with Common Core.

Achieve says: "P-20 Data Systems: States must collect, coordinate, and use K-12 and postsecondary data to track and improve the readiness of graduates to succeed in college and the workplace. Longitudinal data systems should follow individual students from grade to grade and school to school, all the way from kindergarten through postsecondary education and into the workplace."[14] Marc Tucker must be very proud.

NO PARENTS ALLOWED

Given that many of these organizations are federally funded, parents expect access to these meetings. Alas, since these are private groups, the meetings are closed to the public and not subject to the "sunshine" laws.

In October of 2012, a mom in Indiana, Heather Crossin, wanted to attend a CCSSO meeting about Common Core in her hometown. She wanted to listen in on their development of the new Common Core Social Studies standards. (Yes, Common Core Social Studies is coming, as well as Science.) She was told she was not welcome to attend. When she asked for a list of those writing the standards, she was told the names were not available for public release.[15]

These D.C. groups will argue that this was "state-led" and public discourse was fulfilled by placing the standards on their website for public comment. But the standards were posted for comment before anyone outside the education reform circles knew what Common Core was. How could we comment if we didn't know it existed?

They also argue that they incorporated a feedback group of educators and experts from around the country. It's a nice sentiment but far from state-led or local control with statements like this: "Final decisions regarding the Common Core standards document will be made by the Standards Development Work Group. The Feedback Group will play an advisory role, not a decision-making role in the process." If you ask me, giving a handful of teachers a free trip to a conference in D.C. does not qualify as "state-led."[16]

THE COPYRIGHT

Despite the fact that the local reformer lobbyists here in Arkansas refer to the Common Core State Standards as "Arkansas' Standards," the standards do not belong to my state. The individual states did not develop them nor can they alter them without risking *copyright infringement*.

The copyright to the standards belongs to the NGA and CCSSO. According to the Memorandum of Understanding (MOU), the contract the states signed with the CCSSO, states may not alter the standards on their own without risking a copyright violation. States may only add 15% *on top of* the existing standards. Yet, the owners (NGA and CCSSO) refer to the standards as a "living document" that they may change at their discretion. If we thought it was a challenge getting things done at the state level, just imagine doing so with a private group based in D.C.!

BILL GATES

Second only to the U.S. Federal Government, Bill Gates is the largest financier of all things Common Core. Yes, *that* Bill Gates, founder of Microsoft™ and the progressive MSNBC media network.

In 2007, The Bill and Melinda Gates Foundation funded an organization called Common Core Inc. He compares our classrooms to factories and he's funding a program to install surveillance cameras in classrooms to ensure our teachers are in line, making that surveillance part of their evaluations. His goal with Common Core, in his words, is to *"Unleash a powerful market force in the service of better teaching"* and to create *"a large uniform base of customers."* [17]

Since I have taken up this cause, I have yet to see any research that indicates that poor teaching is what plagues our education system. Yet the Gates Foundation is spending millions on teacher retraining and workshops, despite the fact that proponents of Common Core constantly tout that teachers won't have to change what they do in the classroom or how they teach.

The Gates Foundation has financed this initiative to the tune of over $240 million and counting, buying the endorsement of every stakeholder in the education system in advance, including:

- The NGA, the CCSSO and Achieve Inc.
- The U.S. Chamber of Commerce
- The American Federation of Teachers (AFT, teacher union)
- The National Education Association (NEA, teacher union)
- The Fordham Institute
- Scholastic, Inc.
- The National Science Foundation
- Harvard University
- Teach for America

Despite the fact that the national teachers' unions received millions from the Gates Foundation, there is power in numbers and many unions are speaking out against Common Core. In January of 2014, the New York State United Teachers (NYSUT), a union 600,000 strong, *unanimously* opposed Common Core. The following month, the largest national teacher union, the NEA, referred to the implementation of the Common Core as "completely botched," demanding a course correction. In May, the Chicago Teachers Union declared *unanimous* opposition to Common Core. Also in May, the American Federation of Teachers (AFT) offered pushback by declining further money from the Gates Foundation for another controversial reform effort, the Innovation Fund, due to union members expressing opposition to Common Core. [18]

The Gates Foundation also funded state-specific organizations and agencies. I recommend that parents log into the database and see if your state received money directly as well. For instance, in my home state of Arkansas:

- Arkansas Department of Education: $1.9 million
- Arkansas Public School Resource Center Inc. $200,000
- University of Arkansas Fayetteville: $132, 000
- Southern Education Foundation: $500,056
- Arkansas Department of Higher Education: $1,000,000

Why would Gates be involved with K-12 education? Well, for starters, Gates, through his company, Microsoft™, signed a non-governmental cooperative agreement with UNESCO (the United Nations Educational, Scientific and Cultural Organization) in 2004 for the purposes of funding and creating a "*global* education system." Gates says that Microsoft™ "supports the objectives of UNESCO." [19]

So, Gates wants social change and, well, why not make a profit at the same time? I find it interesting that Gates is a college dropout himself. He is not, nor has he ever been a teacher or an education policy-maker. So what are his qualifications? Oh, that's right. He's rich. His solution? Buy the education system!

The United Nations (UN) has come to adore and promote private-public partnerships like the one it has with Microsoft™, for its agendas, especially in education, and even more so when done through a philanthropic arm of the organization. In 1998, the UN's charitable agency, the UN Foundation, was started by Ted Turner of CNN with a $1 billion contribution. Most of the non-government funding for all things Common Core comes from the philanthropic arm of a corporation, thus avoiding wading into the waters of a monopoly. This is all, of course, despite the fact that there is zero research to demonstrate that such partnerships actually work in the education sector, especially on a global level.

Intel™, Cisco™, Harvard University, also signed educational non-government organization agreements with UNESCO as well and conveniently, they are all promoters and contractors of the Common Core.[20] So, big business and the United Nations are working together for global education standards, a managed economy and social change.

JEB BUSH

For a dash of bipartisanship, enter former Governor Jeb Bush. As a member of the NGA and having served as Governor of Florida for eight years, in 2008 he launched a non-profit called the Foundation for Excellence in Education. His organization, promoting the Common Core, is funded by the Bill and Melinda Gates Foundation (with a grant of $5.2 million) and The Walton Family Foundation, among others.

Like many of the rich, elitist proponents of Common Core, he takes a condescending tone with parents who oppose this. Ignoring our real concerns, he says those who oppose Common Core are worried too much about children's self-esteem. He says, "Let me tell you something. In Asia today, they don't care about children's self-esteem. They care about math, whether they can read—in English—whether they understand why science is important, whether they have the grit and determination to be successful," [21]

Bush goes on, "You tell me which society is going to be the winner in this 21st Century: The one that worries about how they feel, or the one that worries about making sure the next generation has the capacity to eat everybody's lunch?" [22]

How much *grit* does it take to be a factory worker in *communist* China? And, can you point out to me, exactly *what*, in the Common Core standards, is going to increase my child's capacity to eat everybody's lunch? That says a lot about Jeb Bush's definition of success in this world. Eat everybody's lunch, indeed.

SIR MICHAEL BARBER AND PEARSON EDUCATION

Sir Michael Barber of England, Chief Education Advisor at Pearson Education, is a self-proclaimed education revolutionary. He used to be the Head of Global Education Practice at McKinsey. If being the head of a global big data firm doesn't send shivers up your spine, he was also a co-chair on the Pakistan Education Task Force and still works on that initiative. In his own education manifesto, *Deliverology 101*, he praises global standards, advocates "sustainable reform" and suggests that Educrats "make it so it can never go back to how it was before" by working on the mindset and the culture of parents and our troublesome "wish for the past." [23]

Based in the U.K., Pearson Education is the largest education company in the world, owner of the *Financial Times* and a contracted testing arm of the Common Core State Standards Initiative. They dominate the education publishing market, operating in 70 countries with 60% of their sales in North America. Most of the publishers we remember from our school days have been swallowed by the Pearson whale, including Penguin, Prentice-Hall and Scott-Foresman.

Just in time for Common Core, in 2010, Pearson announced that it had acquired America's Choice (Marc Tucker's company).[24] One year after the standards were adopted, in 2011, Pearson Education partnered with Microsoft™. Can you say Crony Capitalism? In fact, earlier this year (2014) the two announced that Microsoft™ would be loading Pearson's Common Core materials onto the new Microsoft™ tablets.

Ka-Ching!

We have already established that Gates is accountable to UNESCO. Who is Pearson accountable to? Who are the Pearson shareholders? Almost 3% of the company (24 million shares) is owned by none other than the Libyan Investment Authority (LIA). Do you know who founded the LIA? Seif Al-Islam, the son of dictator and Islamic terrorist Muammar Gaddafi.[25]

Let that one simmer for a minute while you rotate the laundry...

While the LIA assets are "effectively frozen" according to Pearson, the influence behind Pearson is not good news for American textbooks, especially the social studies and history books. Pearson takes a very, shall we say, "across the pond" view of American history and government. In its own words, Pearson says: "Pearson is the world's leading Pre-K-20 educational publishing company, dedicated to working with educators to *change the way America thinks*." (Emphasis added.)[26]

This is the company that Microsoft™ partnered with. There is no doubt in my mind that Pearson Education is dedicated to changing the way my child thinks, in the sense that they wish to change the worldview of an entire generation of Americans. Social change strikes again.

Need examples? No problem.

Exhibit A:

> Claudia Henneberry, a retired teacher in Tennessee, references a Pearson book titled, *American Government and Politics*. She points out that it portrays capitalism as unfair and the wealthy as greedy; furthermore, white, Protestant, conservative and Southern people are described negatively. The phrase "The White South" is used to describe the South. And then there is this divisive passage: "The Democratic Party (after the 1950s) advocated racial integration and other civil rights policies that drove white, Protestant, Southern voters who opposed these initiatives away."[27]

Exhibit B:

> A second outcry in Tennessee resulted in Pearson striking controversial anti-Semitic statements from future editions of another

textbook, this time a geography book titled *The Cultural Landscape*. The book suggested that terrorist attacks against Israeli citizens were legitimate because they were carried out by Palestinians in political retaliation. The text also suggested that the attacks launched by Israel are unprovoked and against ordinary Palestinian citizens. [2829]

Exhibit C:

In Volusia County Florida, *World History,* a book used in an advanced placement class, outraged parents in 2013. The book devoted an entire chapter to Islam, including the rise of Islam and the expansion of the Muslim empire. Which sounds benign, until one notices that other religions such as Christianity and Judaism do not have dedicated chapters and are only sparsely referenced in other sections of the book. [30]

Exhibits D and E:

Thank goodness for national activist groups like The Textbook League that identified two other Pearson books, *Across the Centuries* and *World Cultures: A Global Mosaic,* as filled with Islamic doctrine presented as factual information.

Exhibit F:

This Pearson "grammar" lesson angered parents around the nation with statements like: "[The president] makes sure the laws of the country are fair," "The wants of an individual are less important than the well-being of the nation" and "The commands of government officials must be obeyed by all." [31]

Pearson's influence doesn't stop at textbooks. Pearson is also the Common Core-contracted vendor to offer the new computer-based assessments (standardized tests). Despite the fact that Pearson calls its influence in education a "charitable mission," they hold billions in contracts for Common Core implementation and profit each time a student takes an exam. For instance, their contract with 14 states through The Partnership for the Readiness of College and Careers (PARCC) is worth $240 million *a year* to test up to 10 million students annually. In New York, Pearson's testing contract alone is worth $35 million. In Texas, Pearson has a 5-year, $500 million testing contract. [32]

Pearson Education has been under fire for incomplete and incorrect materials, faulty test scores, faulty test questions and illegal contract negotiations. Pearson was recently fined $7 million for "accidentally making a profit" with its charitable arm. They also paid $15 million in fines to the State of Florida.[33]

Check out the laundry list of Pearson incompetence I've reproduced in *Appendix A*, as reported by Valerie Strauss in the Washington Post, with over 32 infractions. Why any state would do business with this amateurish vendor is beyond me. After looking at that list, I cannot imagine my child being held accountable to one of the high-stakes exams provided and scored by Pearson Education. [34]

Considering the rhetoric in their textbooks, I am also concerned as a parent about the passages my children will read when they take a Pearson test. Parents and teachers are not allowed to preview the testing materials. In fact, teachers and students are expected to sign confidentiality agreements instead.

In addition to providing the platform for the online tests, Pearson also competes with other big data corporations for the workforce steering part of the reform. The student data gathered from the assessments will be used to create a career track for students.

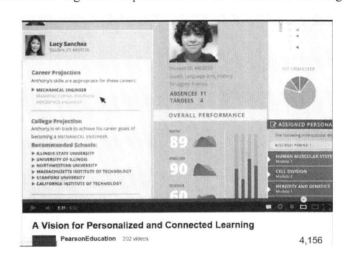

A Vision for Personalized and Connected Learning

PearsonEducation   202 videos   4,156

But wait, there's more!

Pearson also offers a new teacher evaluation system called Teacher Performance Assessment (TPA). More on that later. They are also now wading into healthcare waters with a new test for Attention Deficit Hyperactive Disorder. Given their history, I find *that* truly scary.

RUPERT MURDOCH AND NEWS CORP

If your state participates in the AIR/Smarter Balanced Assessment Consortium (SBAC), the elitist developing your assessments is Rupert Murdoch, media mogul and executive Chair of News Corp. Amplify Insight, part of News Corp, snagged a $12.5 million contract from SBAC for the assessments. Remember that the CCSSO (Council of Chief State School Officers) partnered with Amplify. (By now, you probably feel like you're wading through alphabet soup, but please, stay with me!)

AIR is also funded by progressive investor, George Soros and his Open Society initiative.

Murdoch echoes Bill Gates when he identifies the market transformation and the service of great teaching saying, "When it comes to K through 12 education, we see a $500 billion sector in the U.S. alone that is waiting desperately to be transformed by big breakthroughs that extend the reach of great teaching." [35]

Murdoch and his newspapers are facing a myriad of criminal and corporate charges from the FBI and Scotland Yard in London for international phone hacking, targeting thousands of people. As I write this, the Crown Prosecution Service wants to interview Murdoch as a suspect in conspiring to intercept communications. [36]

This is not an isolated event. In English Civil and Criminal Court, Murdoch is mired in over a dozen cases so far. Investigators have arrested or interviewed over 100 journalists from six of Murdoch's publications. Also, in Scotland, three of his journalists, face trials on charges of perjury, phone hacking and breach of data protection laws. So far, Murdoch has settled and paid damages to over 700 victims.

Parents are just supposed to look the other way when a company like this is responsible for our children's student data and testing? We're supposed to trust the future of our children to international business moguls this tainted by corruption?

CONFLICT OF INTEREST

According to IBIS Capital, a London-based banking firm, the global education market is worth $4.4 trillion, with K-12 education making up

50% of that amount and post-secondary making up 34%. It is considered the fastest growing sector for venture capitalists and is expected to get bigger with increasing privatization of our school system.[37]

The fundamental fork in the road here lies with accountability and a *clear conflict of interest*. Private corporations are not accountable to voters or *parents*; rather they are accountable to shareholders. *Shareholders expect* profits, *not exceptional test scores or well-educated individuals.*

The Appleton Chamber of Commerce held a presentation in Wisconsin promoting Common Core. When parents asked about being included in the reform, they were told, "We did not include them because we did not know how this would work... *We are not telling the parents; their children will bring them along.*" [38] Professor Thomas Newkirk of New Hampshire echoes the concerns of parents when he reminds us that,

> It is a fundamental principle of governance that those who establish the guidelines, do not benefit financially from those guidelines," arguing that this is exactly why we do not allow pharmaceutical companies to set healthcare guidelines. Yet, in the case of taxpayer-funded education, which rides on federal and state mandates, we now have the opposite. [39]

Aside from lack of accountability, here is the conflict of interest: For capitalists like Gates, Pearson and Murdoch, success is defined in terms of profits and profits come from fulfilling a perceived need in the system. The only way they will have sustained revenue is if there is always a crisis or problem to be solved. And a crisis justifies federal interference. Therefore, there will always be an education "crisis."

Chapter

5

The Fundamental Increase of the Federal Role

"The philosophy in the schoolroom in one generation, will be the philosophy in the government in the next."
~ Abraham Lincoln

In addition to funding private interest groups, the federal government, namely the U.S. Department of Education (DOE), has significantly increased its role in "state-led" education. Of course, this is not news. U.S. Secretary of Education Arne Duncan was just more outspoken and blunt about it than others have been before him. The federal government has been involved in education since the colonial days of the late 1700s.

It started with federal land grants for schools known as the Land and Northwest Ordinances. Then came tax code incentives and bonds. In 1917, Congress passed the Smith-Hughes Act, which added vocational education to the curriculum, due to increased immigration.

During the wave of starvation resulting from WWII, Congress started subsidizing school lunches. Of course, I believe this was more to produce strong troops than it was to aid students.

The 1950s brought desegregation with Brown v. Board of Education. The 1960s brought the Individuals with Disabilities Act and The General Education Provisions Act. The 1970s brought Title IX of the Education Amendments of 1972, which broadened opportunities for women in athletics programs in schools. All these notable mandates of fairness and liberty were enacted without the government changing what was taught or how. For that, you need a crisis. Enter the "Nation at Risk" report card issued in 1983.

As is the case with every other federal program, the scope of government involvement expanded and evolved into something much bigger and more intrusive. Everything changed in the 1980s. The United States Department of Education was established in 1980, under the Department of Education Organization Act, to establish accountability to Congress. This created a department separate from the office of Health, Education and Welfare. It passed the house with a very narrow majority.

Until this point, the federal government's interference was limited to civil rights and funding, with strings attached, of course. Soon, the first government-funded assessment was created. The Educational Testing Service and the National Assessment of Education Progress (NAEP) were ushered in along with the Nation at Risk Report in 1983.

In the 1990s, the Clinton Administration made education about the economy, about developing corporate serfs instead of creating a free citizenry. This is also when national standards became the latest topic of controversy, with attempts to establish them failing miserably.

At the turn of the 21st century, the second President Bush gave us the mega-testing, outcome-based education effort called No Child Left Behind. Now, with the Common Core State Standards Initiative, we have No Child Left Behind revived and on steroids.

BREAKING THE LAW

The reformers and supporters of CCSSI will say it is an issue of semantics but those who know their history know that this reform is a violation of federal law. It specifically violates three federal mandates as well as the Tenth Amendment.

Fortunately, back in 1965, when the federal government made that first critical step into the classroom with the *General Education Provisions Act*, legislators foresaw what could happen generations later. So they placed amendments into the laws in an effort to protect us:

1965 Elementary and Secondary Education Act

"Nothing in this Act shall be construed to authorize an officer or employee of the Federal Government to mandate, direct, or control a State, local educational agency, or school's curriculum, program of instruction, or allocation of State and local resources..."

1970 General Education Provisions Act

"No provision of any applicable program shall be construed to authorize any department, agency, officer, or employee of the United States to exercise any direction, supervision, or control over the curriculum, program of instruction, administration, or personnel of any educational institution, school, or school system..."

1979 Department of Education Organization Act

No provision of a program administered by the Secretary or by any other officer of the Department shall be construed to authorize the Secretary or any such officer to exercise any direction, supervision, or control over the curriculum, program of instruction, administration, or personnel of any educational institution, school, or school system, over any accrediting agency or association, or over the selection or content of library resources, textbooks, or other instructional materials by any educational institution or school system, except to the extent authorized by law.

Despite these federal laws, the US Department of Education now uses the waiver from the worst provisions of No Child Left Behind to coerce states into adopting common standards, and provides the funding for the standards, the tests and the databases.

The Tenth Amendment of the US Constitution declares, "The powers not delegated to the United States by the Constitution, nor prohibited by it to the States, are reserved to the States respectively, or to the people." As such, education has always been a state responsibility and should remain so without federal control coming in the form of financial threats.

U.S. SECRETARY OF EDUCATION ARNE DUNCAN

In a 2009 interview with Charlie Rose, brand new U.S. Secretary of Education Arne Duncan said he wanted government schools to become the "center of community life," open 12-14 hours a day, 6-7 days per week, and host to all the students' extra-curricular activities, including family meals and health clinics.[40]

This was coming from someone who majored in Sociology and played basketball for a living. He ran the Chicago Public School system while he made friends playing ball with then would-be President Obama. This man doesn't have an education degree and he has never taught in a classroom in his life. [41]

When parents speak out about Common Core, after being told for years that we're too uninvolved in our children's education, Duncan makes racially and socially divisive statements about white suburban mothers who are disappointed that our kids aren't as brilliant as we thought they were. Suddenly, parents should be seen and not heard, an ironic example of bully bandwagon culture from the Department of Education. [42] But to be fair, Duncan inherited this mess to some degree, arriving when the reform was already on a fixed trajectory from the Clinton and G.W. Bush Administrations.

CONGRESS BYPASSED

Before Common Core, standards and other education decisions were handled in the public forum of the state legislature, with great public discourse, and were subject to the Freedom of Information Act (also known as the sunshine laws providing public record). Reforms that affected the states as a whole, such as testing, data and grants, were handled in Congress. Common Core did not go through Congress, under the guise that it was "voluntary" for the states (despite the looming NCLB waiver threat). In 2013, angry members of Congress sent a letter up to Arne Duncan voicing concern about it. The letter voiced Congressional concern over bypassing Congress, making changes to federal data and disbursement policies, and called Common Core a one-size-fits-all program that does not meet the needs of the individual states.[43]

The public can sit in on Congressional meetings and submit requests for information under the Freedom of Information Act. Since the legislative process was bypassed with Common Core, our voice was silenced, once again, this time on the federal level.

UNESCO (UNITED NATIONS EDUCATIONAL, SCIENTIFIC AND CULTURAL ORGANIZATION) CONNECTION

It turns out that multinational corporations like Microsoft™, Intel™ and Cisco™ aren't the only ones who signed a cooperative agreement with UNESCO. In 2003, George W. Bush signed the United States on as well.

Thanks to former education secretary Margaret Spellings, the U.S. also signed the Moscow Declaration. In it, "Ministers recognized that the internationalization of education is a reality." It then calls for an education system "…implemented by education ministers of all the world countries and international organizations, including the World Bank, UNESCO, and U.N." The U.S. "pledged to share best practices across borders" to build "education systems that can allow people… to live and contribute to a *global society, and to work in a global economy*" [44]

This is all part and parcel of the "Decade of Education for Sustainable Development," the purpose of which is to "integrate the values inherent in sustainable development into all aspects of training, to encourage changes in behaviour that will enable a more viable and fairer society for everyone." Did you notice the words training, behavior and fair? This is a Neo-liberal love fest for redistribution and social equity, and heck, why not make a profit at the same time?

Sure, they work to get an education for girls in third world countries and Gates loves to give them free electronic tablets. UNESCO believes the way to peace, sustainable development and a stable global economy starts with standardized, outcome-based education for the masses.

What are the education objectives of UNESCO?

UNESCO favors global standards and a curriculum that utilizes constructivism (self directed learning, more on that in Chapter 5), in the name of peace. This excerpt from the UN's "Peace Education: Framework for Teacher Education (2005)," demonstrates their praise for individual data collection and standardized assessments:

"For assessing the covert behaviour, it may be necessary to use a set of psychological instruments like attitude scale, different types of inventories, and tests of personality on aggression, etc. One important tool for assessing change in the student behaviour will be careful observation against a properly design observation schedule for each student, documenting incidences of violent behaviour vis-à-vis peace behaviour like cooperation, mutual help, conflict resolution, etc. The change in behaviour is a slow and steady process; hence it has to be observed over a period of time. Each school therefore, has to develop a blueprint for assessment of students on peace values and behaviour. Such a blueprint should have provision for maintaining records of observation as well as results of psychological tests in the pattern of a cumulative record card or a portfolio. Such records can be maintained in computers."[45]

As part of an older UNESCO 10-part teacher training module in 1949 called Towards World Understanding, Vol. V: In the Classroom with Children Under Thirteen Years of Age: "As long as the child breathes the poisoned air of nationalism, education in world-mindedness can produce only rather precarious results. As we have pointed out, it is frequently the family that infects the child with extreme nationalism. The school should therefore use the means described earlier to combat family attitudes that favor jingoism." [46]

It is no wonder that so many of our materials, especially those published by Pearson, place more emphasis on the U.N. Declaration of Human Rights over the U.S. Bill of Rights, preach environmental policies and raise social justice issues as early as kindergarten. The idea of removing nationalism and sacrificing individualism in the name of the global community is completely *U.N.*-American.

Looking at other members of UNESCO, many countries are also undergoing almost identical education reforms as the U.S., establishing common standards and assessments in the name of this new world order Vice President Biden keeps bragging about. Australia just went through an almost identical education reform, and Barry McGaw, Chair of the Australian Curriculum, Assessment and Reporting Authority, was a member of the CCSS Validation Committee. Canada is fighting fuzzy math with provincial petitions and parents in Malaysia recently complained of product placement in and data mining of their student assessments.

The Common Core and its associated reforms are part of a multinational effort to standardize education globally in the name of peace, profit and sustainability. This is not what America wants. I'm not saying that we are not aware that we have to work together with other countries and play nice in the sandbox, or that we are not culturally aware. I'm saying that we love our country and wish to take care of our own business and be free. Moreover, if we think it is difficult getting things done at the state or federal level, just imagine trying to influence policies that are executed by private corporations at the global level! How are parents and teachers supposed to direct the education of our children? What choices will we have? Will our voices be heard then?

As part of our agreement with UNESCO, our United States Secretary of Education makes a speech to the UNESCO conference each year. The 2009 and 2010 speeches from Secretary Arne Duncan are worth reading. In his 2010 speech, he refers to our students as "human capital" and vows to reform education in America to fulfill workforce needs instead of creating innovative thinkers or intellectuals with free minds. Duncan says, "Our goal for the coming year will be to work closely with global partners, including UNESCO, to promote qualitative improvements and system-strengthening... That goal can only be achieved by creating a strong *cradle-to-career* continuum that starts with early childhood learning and extends all the way to *college and careers*." Then he takes the Obama Administration an unprecedented step further when he makes this stunning remark to UNESCO, "The Obama administration has sought to *fundamentally shift the federal role*..." (Emphasis added.).[47] And shift the federal role they did, from the cradle to the grave, with $4.35 *billion* dollars in taxpayer-provided stimulus money for the states.

RACE TO THE TOP OF CAPITAL HILL

When President Obama took office in 2009, he built upon the foundation laid by every administration that came before him and in March announced the Race to the Top (RttT) reform initiative. If states could demonstrate their willingness to adopt federal reforms, he would show them the money. States had to act fast as this was a limited time offer and a competition. Not every state would win. Cash strapped states jumped at the chance to win a piece of the $4.35 billion pie.

Participating in RttT also meant a waiver from some of the worst provisions of No Child Left Behind (NCLB). The NCLB reform that came from the G.W. Bush administration was horrific for many states, ushering in outcome-based education, teaching to the test, cheating schemes, states lowering their standards to appear to be achieving and school closings due to low test scores. For many states, despite being in a fiscal recession, the NCLB waiver carried more incentive than the grant money.

The NCLB Waiver document describes how a state—to be eligible for the waiver—must adopt standards common to a "significant" number of states. Well, as I mentioned earlier, the NGA and CCSSO just "happen" to hold the copyright on a set of standards, commonly known as the Common Core State Standards (CCSS).

States also had to agree to individual student data collection, using that data to inform instruction and to continuously improve. This required setting up a system that "produces student achievement data and student growth data that can be used to determine whether individual students are college- and career-ready or on track to being college- and career-ready… and produces data... that can be used to inform: [list of uses]…"[48] It's a race and Big Brother is chasing you!

THE FOUR ASSURANCES OF REFORM

In his speech to UNESCO, Secretary Arne Duncan outlined *The Four Assurances* of reform. The states were expected to fulfill these items, which were assigned varying numbers of points to be awarded, in the Race to the Top Application.[49]

REFORM ASSURANCE #1

Adopting *standards and assessments* that prepare students to succeed in college and the workplace and to compete in the global economy.

REFORM ASSURANCE #2

Building *data systems* that measure student growth and success, and inform teachers and principals about how they can improve instruction.

REFORM ASSURANCE #3

Recruiting, developing, rewarding and retaining *effective teachers and principals*, especially where they are needed most.

REFORM ASSURANCE #4

Turning around our *lowest-achieving schools*.

Later, I will discuss these assurances in depth. But first, let me tell you what happened right after RttT was announced in March 2009. This application and approval process happened *very* quickly, leaving little time for public, state-led discourse or research. Not to worry! Bill Gates was ready with $2.7 million dollars in resources to help states quickly prepare their 300-page proposals, chock-full of biased research he also funded.

In March 2010, the second draft of CCSS is released. On April 14, 2010, Stage II applications for RttT funding, requiring states to commit to adopting "a common set of K–12 standards by August 2, 2010," are due. Then on June 2, 2010, the final Common Core State Standards are published.[50] The Arkansas State Board of Education adopted the standards on behalf of the state of Arkansas in July of 2010.

The contract was due in April, but the standards weren't complete until June? Don't worry, we're the U.S. DOE and we are here to help you. We promise the standards are rigorous, college-ready and will prepare your kids for a global economy!

Alaska, North Dakota, Texas and Vermont did not take the bait, refusing to enter the "race." Only 19 states "won" the Race to the Top. But regardless of whether a state "won" the race, it was *still obligated* to the commitments made in the RttT agreement, which is why so many states adopted the CCSSI even though they did not get RttT grant funds. Note: Standards and Assessments were worth 70 out of 500 total points on the application.

My home state, Arkansas, did not win RttT grant money, per se. Instead, Arkansas received $363 million in State Fiscal Stabilization Funds (SFSF). The Common Core Propaganda Parade likes to say that our state did not get money in exchange for the Common Core standards. This is not quite true.

States were required to have the SFSF approved to be *considered* for the RttT grant. According to the U.S. DOE, the SFSF is: "a new, *one-time* appropriation of approximately $48.6 billion that the U.S. Department of Education (Department) will award to Governors to help stabilize State and local budgets to minimize and avoid reductions in education and other essential services, in exchange for a State's commitment to advance essential education reform in four areas:

"(1) Making *improvements in teacher effectiveness* and in the equitable distribution of qualified teachers for all students, particularly students who are most in need;

(2) establishing *pre-K-to-college-and-career data systems* that track progress and foster continuous improvement;

(3) making progress toward *rigorous college- and career-ready standards and high-quality assessments* that are valid and reliable for all students, including limited English proficient students and students with disabilities; and

(4) providing targeted, intensive support and effective interventions for the lowest-performing schools." (Emphasis added.)[51]

Those are the Four Assurances! Further, according to www.ed.gov: "States must report their progress toward completing these assurances in their applications to receive money under the $48.6 billion State Fiscal Stabilization Fund. The Department of Education will evaluate states' success in meeting the four assurances when considering states' applications for competitive grants under the $4.35 billion Race to the Top Fund."[52] Sounds like Common Core to me...

FROM THE CRADLE TO THE GRAVE

States that won the RttT Early Learning Challenge portion of the grant program agreed to develop standards for preschoolers that align with K-3 in the name of creating a true P-20 (individual preschool to age 20) system of education. The "winners" were California, Delaware, Maryland, Massachusetts, North Carolina, Ohio, Rhode Island and Washington. [53]

This does not sit well with me. First of all, where are they taking us? It may be voluntary at first, and seem like a welcome idea to working parents who would appreciate free full-time daycare for their toddlers. But what starts out as voluntary or "just a pilot program" often becomes the status quo or a federal mandate later on, especially in education. Already ACT is developing a career aptitude test for kindergarteners. *For kindergarteners.* Really. Come *on.*

When she grows up and has children of her own, I do not want my daughter being told she has to hand over a three- or four-year-old child to a government school. The school should *not* be the center of community life—that is family. Instead of encouraging young mothers to think they should hand their babies over to the state, we should be strengthening families, and promoting play for toddlers

Finland is number one in PISA (see Note below) education circles. This is despite the fact that they do not emphasize standardized testing and do not enroll children in school until age seven. The kids finish by age 16 and then go on to college-level academic study or vocation study.

Do you know what country starts with infant school at one year of age? China.

> **Note**: PISA is the Program for International Student Assessment, a test administered every three years by the Organization for Economic Cooperation and Development. The OECD is a group of 30 member countries, including the U.S., which discusses and develops economic and social policy.

Chapter

6

State-Led or State Burden?

*"Whensoever the general government assumes undelegated powers...
a nullification of the act is the rightful remedy."*
~ *Thomas Jefferson*

Despite hundreds of millions in stimulus money, the states do not receive enough federal money to cover the overall cost of implementing the Common Core initiative. The Fordham Institute projects that Arkansas will spend $153 million of its own money on implementation. Once the stimulus grants run out, it is up to the states to produce funding for materials, continuing education, computer bandwidth, etc. Rather than a state-led effort, this is really another unfunded mandate.

Sarah Reckhow, an expert in philanthropy and education policy at Michigan State University, points out:

> Usually, there's a pilot test—something is tried on a small scale, outside researchers see if it works, and then it's promoted on a broader scale... That didn't happen with the Common Core. Instead, they aligned the research with the advocacy... At the end of the day, it's going to be the states and local districts that pay for this.[54]

The definition of state-led is different for the reformers than it is for the parents. The term state-led conveys to me, as a parent and taxpayer, that the initiative was voted on in the state legislature with open debate and public discourse. The reformers argue that "state-led" is fulfilled with two signatures: that of an appointed state school commissioner and a governor. I submit that this reform initiative is not state-led; it is corporate-led by elitist corporations and special interest groups. Even David Coleman of Achieve described his task as trying to "convince" governors to adopt these standards. If the states were leading this initiative, doesn't it seem strange that they would need convincing?[55]

Jim Sturgios of the Pioneer Institute argues that the Common Core profiteers, "misunderstand the kind of transparency, effort and public deliberation associated with the development of academic standards by states." He goes on to describe how the successful Massachusetts standards were developed: "In Massachusetts, public consideration of our state standards in the late 1990s and early 2000s included drafts developed after extensive parent, teacher, scholarly and business input; extensive public comment periods; public hearings; extensive revisions, which were again put out for public comment. Throughout the entire process, the state's Board of Education provided oversight and input on the process; it was discussed at public Board meetings. Throughout the process the state's Department of Education provided technical support and direction. The development of standards and tests was on the front pages of our newspapers for years. As a result, parents and teachers had an opportunity to follow and participate in the debate; they saw the controversies; and they could ultimately feel ownership of some very difficult and far-reaching reforms." [56]

Did the Common Core Initiative bear any resemblance to this process? No. That's why, now, five years later, with angry parents, frightened and frustrated teachers and confused lawmakers, we are finally having the public discourse that should have taken place back in 2008.

The damage is done. Our kids will never get these years back. The federal strings are a tangled mess and the states are left with the burden of cost as well as trying to figure out how to unravel this nightmare of a reform initiative that is experimenting on our kids. I think of Sir Michael Barber and his "sustainable reform" and wish for the past, 40 years ago, when we had true local control and a high degree of college attainment.

Those who are not quite ready to take a stance against Common Core will point their fingers at the implementation, rather than the initiative itself. They throw our beloved teachers and superintendents under the bus for a failed rollout. The reality is that in another sense this is once again more than standards. Sure, the reform stinks, but often the cognitive dissonance on the part of the stakeholders makes it a bitter pill to swallow. Researchers, administrators, investors, etc. who plunged years of hard work, millions of dollars and good intentions into our education policies, and loyalty to their employer, now find themselves aligned with individuals and ideologies that are in conflict with their conscience and with what is best for our kids and our America.

It's not the implementation. Or, let me clarify. It's not the fault of the hands-on teachers and administrators in the trenches. They and the local school districts, in most states, have very little control over the implementation. Their marching orders come from the ever-overreaching arms of the state boards of education and the federal government.

When we call for a repeal, or at least a moratorium, the Common Core Propaganda Parade argues that too much money has been spent putting it into place. They say that too much blood, sweat and tears have been poured into it. That's like saying we shouldn't put out a raging fire because so much money was spent on the kindling.

Chapter

7

Assurance #1: National, I Mean, Common Standards and Assessments

"We are raising today's children in sterile, risk-averse and highly structured environments. In so doing, we are failing to cultivate artists, pioneers and entrepreneurs, and instead cultivating a generation of children who can follow the rules in organized sports games, sit for hours in front of screens and mark bubbles on standardized tests."
~ Darell Hammond

When the Common Core was adopted in 2010, only the English Language Arts (ELA) and Math Standards were available. As I write this, the Social Studies and Next Generation Science standards are being drafted. Let's look at those existing standards, starting with the ELA standards.

COMMON STANDARDS

English Language Arts (ELA) Standards

The ELA standards are more than English, or rather, anything but English. According to the standards, ELA includes Social Studies, History and Technical Studies. They call for 50%-70% informational text in lieu of established literature. [57]

Upon calling our own Arkansas Department of Education on this matter, *Arkansas Against Common Core* was told how important it was that our children learn to read manuals, especially since the person we spoke with over the telephone was struggling with putting together a swing set for her kids.

I will give you a moment to pick your jaw up off the floor...

Informational texts include books, magazines, handouts, brochures and Internet articles that aren't always credible sources. Most reflect some form of media spin, with content leaning to one side. Established literature, however, has stood the test of time in education around the *world*, because it teaches students *how* to think, not *what* to think.

Often, informational text is lumped in with non-fiction when parents and educators debate the pros and cons of an emphasis on informational text. Keep in mind, this model of education is workforce- and social justice-driven, therefore the type of informational text is specific.

This is different from other works of non-fiction such as reference materials or biographies. Scholastic, despite being a Gates-paid shill for Common Core, offers an excellent clarification of informational text for teachers: "The primary purpose of informational text is to *convey infor-*

mation about the natural or social world, typically by someone presumed to know." (Emphasis added.) [58]

Sounds like a nod to global social justice and behavior to me. A study was done by the Institute of Educational Sciences National Center for Education Statistics in 2008 that supports the argument that literature is more effective than informational text. It was called *The Reading Literacy of Fourth Grade Students in International Contexts.* It found that students who read stories or novels scored 4% *higher* than the *international* average and those who read informational texts scored 2% *lower* than *international* average.

Further, as parents, we have found many of these Common Core-aligned informational texts to be politically charged, anti-American, inappropriate and full of grammatical and sentence structure errors. We have examples to share. Clearly, the ELA standards were *not* internationally benchmarked, as the CCSSO would have us believe.

The guidelines call for students to "stay within the four corners of the text" which is the exact opposite of the critical thinking skills that Mr. and Ms. Common Core say are encouraged by the literacy standards. Staying within the four corners of the text does not permit the reader to apply existing knowledge or experience to the reading, instead analyzing it at face value.[59] In other words, make literal interpretations of narratives, don't think outside the box or offer your own interpretation of a given situation or character. Just do as you are told.

Coleman and Pimentel turn away from narrative writing, instead placing emphasis on persuasive and argumentative essays.[60] In other words, here is what we want you to think, now make an argument for it.

This kind of education will result in a generation of students who lose imagination, innovation and creativity, which I discuss later as the skills needed to compete in the ever-elusive "21st Century Global Economy."

According to clinical psychologist Mark Turner, "Narrative imagining—story—is the fundamental instrument of thought. Rational capacities depend on it. It is our chief means of looking into the future, of predicting, of planning, of explaining." Backing away from literature, and then limiting what our students take away from it and the informational texts they are bombarded with, clearly develops a different kind of human being, one that lacks individuality or questions anything. [61]

The Common Core offers a recommended "Exemplar" reading list. While this list is not mandatory (yet), there are some selections on this list that say a lot about the educational ideology of those shoving this reform down our throats. It has some controversial selections, complete with sexually explicit language and product placement, such as:

- *Dreaming in Cuban*
- *The Bluest Eye*
- Google Hacks: Tips and Tools for Smarter Searching
- U.S. General Services Administration Executive Order 13423: Strengthening Federal Environmental, Energy, and Transportation Management
- Gawande, Atul. "The Cost Conundrum: Health Care Costs in McAllen, Texas." The New Yorker June 1, 2009

Let's start with *Dreaming in Cuban*. It is on the exemplar list and recommended for 10th grade reading. A high school that took this advice had students read the book aloud in class. Parents were outraged. Let me warn you—you may find the passages from *Dreaming in Cuban* and *The Bluest Eye* offensive. (I know I did.) Here is an excerpt from page 80:

Hugo and Felicia stripped in their room, dissolving easily into one another, and made love against the whitewashed walls. Hugo bit Felicia's breast and left purplish bands of bruises on her upper thighs. He knelt before her in the tub and massaged black Spanish soap between her legs. He entered her repeatedly from behind. Felicia learned what pleased him. She tied his arms above his head with their underclothing and slapping him sharply when he asked. 'You're my bi***,' Hugo said, groaning.[62]

Now on to *The Bluest Eye*, recommended for 11th graders, which takes the reader into the perspective of an incestuous child rapist. These excerpts have been slightly edited for language. Pages 162-163:

A bolt of desire ran down his genitals...and softening the lips of his anus... He wanted to f*** her—tenderly. But the tenderness would not hold. The tightness of her vagina was more than he could bear. His soul seemed to slip down his guts and fly out into her, and the gigantic thrust he made into her then provoked the only sound she made. Removing himself from her was so painful to him he cut it short and snatched his genitals out of the dry harbor of her vagina. She appeared to have fainted.

Pages 148-149:

With a violence born of total helplessness, he pulled her dress up, lowered his trousers and underwear. 'I said get on wid it. An'make it good, ni****, Come on c***. Faster. You ain't doing nothing for her.' He almost wished he could do it—hard, long, and painfully, he hated her so much.[63]

Oh, my.

While the Google Hacks selection may provide useful knowledge on searching for information on the internet, it is clearly advertising and not what most parents would consider exemplar high school reading. Further, the government propaganda disguised as higher order reading on this list is disappointing and partisan to say the least. Again, while this list is not mandatory, it says a great deal about the education philosophies of those writing and sponsoring the Common Core standards.

Aside from reading manuals, this about-face on established literature pummels our children with opinionated articles and narratives from U.N.-credible sources with themes of social justice, politics and citizenship. Now, in this brave new *Common Core* world, that is referred to as "literacy" in *English* class. Throw in the Pearson monopoly of materials full of revisionist history and our kids are coming home with narratives that hail Gorbachev as the hero for the fall of the Berlin wall and call Hugo Chavez of Venezuela a liberator. [64]

While some classes, such as Science, call for informational text by nature, applying this across the board of subject matter opens the door to the unintended consequences of indoctrination and the pushing of social agendas in the classroom. Also, let's not forget that English and Literature teachers are trained to teach from established literature.

Established literature promotes critical thinking and literacy with complex vocabulary, varying settings of culture, time and place, and characters immersed in complex situations the reader can identify with. Literature contains the great stories of our history, leaders and culture. Emphasizing informational text tells students what to think, not how to think. To quote Professor Terrance Moore from Hillsdale College, "He who controls the stories, controls the regime." [65]

Speaking of college professors, Dr. Sandra Stotsky, who was on the CCSSI validation committee of 29, was one of five who refused to sign off on the standards. Her credentials put David Coleman to shame. She is Professor of Education Reform in the Department of Education Reform at the University of Arkansas, holding the 21st Century Chair in Teacher Quality, and was the Senior Associate Commissioner in the Massachusetts Department of Education from 1999 to 2003. She is also a professor emeritus at Stanford. She has years of classroom teaching experience.

Dr. Stotsky refused to sign off on the standards, calling them an empty skill set. She says, "Everyone was willing to believe that the Common Core standards are 'rigorous,' 'competitive,' 'internationally benchmarked,' and 'research-based.' They are not." [66]

She explains:

One aspect of the ELA standards that remained untouchable despite the consistent criticisms I sent to the standards writers, was David Coleman's idea that nonfiction or informational texts should occupy at least half of the readings in every English class, to the detriment of classic literature and of literary study more broadly speaking. Even though all the historical and empirical evidence weighed against this concept, his idea was apparently set in stone. [67]

According to Stotsky:

The "lead" writers for the grade-level ELA standards, David Coleman and Susan Pimentel, had never taught reading or English in K-12 or at the college level. Neither has a doctorate in English. Neither has published serious work on K-12 curriculum and instruction. At the time of their appointment, they were unknown to English and reading educators and to higher education faculty in rhetoric, speech, composition or literary study.

Two of the lead grade-level standards-writers in mathematics did have relevant academic credentials but no K-12 teaching experience. Jason Zimba was a physics professor at Bennington College at the time, while William McCallum was (and remains) a mathematics professor at the University of Arizona. The only member of this three-person team with K-12 teaching experience, Phil Daro, had majored in English as an undergraduate; he was also on the staff of NCEE (Marc Tucker's organization). None had ever developed K-12 mathematics standards before. [68]

Once again, we have a small group of elitist individuals, without relevant experience or expertise, making decisions for the rest of the country. And once again, our children are suffering for it.

THE MATH STANDARDS

As illustrated in the Caveman Math story, the most obvious issue for most parents, especially those of 3rd and 4th grade students, is the lack of rote memorization. The only reference to this in the standards is found here where it states that third graders are only expected to memorize the tables for two single digit factors. Here is how rote memorization is outlined in the CCSS:

> ## CCSS.MATH.CONTENT.3.OA.C.7
> Fluently multiply and divide within 100, using strategies such as the relationship between multiplication and division (*e.g.*, knowing that 8 × 5 = 40, one knows 40 ÷ 5 = 8) or properties of operations.
> By the end of Grade 3, know from memory all products of **two** one-digit numbers.

Multiply and divide within 100.[69]

Only two numbers? So rote memorization wasn't entirely removed, it was just gutted down to two numbers.

Other concrete operations and concepts were left out as well. According to the **American Principles Project**, overall, the standards are 1-2 grades behind international peers and they offer a laundry list of missing skills:

* Leaves out prime factorization, least common denominators or greatest common factors; conversions among fractions, decimals, and percent.

* De-emphasizes algebraic manipulation, a prerequisite for advanced mathematics, and instead effectively redefines algebra as "functional algebra," which does not prepare students for STEM (Science, Technology, Engineering and Math) careers.

- Does not require proficiency with addition and subtraction until grade 4.

- Does not require proficiency with multiplication using the standard algorithm until grade 5.

- Does not require proficiency with division using the standard algorithm until grade 6.

- Starts teaching decimals only in grade 4, about two years behind the more rigorous state standards.

- Fails to use money as a natural introduction to this concept.

- Fails to teach in K-8 about key geometrical concepts such as the area of a triangle, sum of angles in a triangle, isosceles and equilateral triangles or constructions with a straightedge and compass.[70]

This echoes the concerns of Dr. James Milgram, professor emeritus from Stanford University and former NASA Advisory Member. He was also one of 5 on the 29-member validation committee that refused to sign off on the standards, He says, "…the reason I didn't sign off on them was that they did not match up to international expectations. They were at least 2 years behind the practices in the high achieving countries by the 7th grade, and… only require a partial understanding of what would be the content of a normal, solid, course in Algebra I or Geometry… Moreover, they cover very little of the content of Algebra 2, and none of any higher-level course… They will not help our children match up to the students in the top foreign countries when it comes to being hired to top level jobs."[71]

Ze'ev Wurman (a U.S. Department of Education official) was also on the validation committee and refused to sign off on the standards. He also found the CCSS leaves students *1-2 years* **behind** *the 2008 National Mathematics Advisory Panel's* recommendations. (Emphasis added.) [72]

The Not-So-New Math: Constructivism

"For, after all, how do we know that two and two make four? Or that the force of gravity works? Or that the past is unchangeable? If both the past and the external world exist only in the mind, and if the mind itself is controllable—what then?"- George Orwell, 1984

I embarked on a path of research regarding this strange new math and found it really wasn't new at all. When I spoke of it to those in the Baby Boomer generation, they recalled the "New Math" of the 1960s when reformers tried to introduce abstract math using the Sputnik Space Race as a "crisis" to justify their experimentation with public school children back then. The parents resisted and it was pushed out in two years. Now the "crisis" is China and the mysterious "21st Century Global Economy."

The language in the Common Core State Standards (CCSS) calls for controversial reform math, otherwise known as constructivist math. Language that calls for students to *explain, argue,, justify, construct, draw diagrams or pictures,* and consider math in an "abstract way" are constructivist/reform math standards. To make matters worse, they are presented as word problems that often do not fit the student's reading level. Also, instead of traditional Euclidean geometry the CCSSI calls for transformational geometry, another type of reform math based on abstract thought, which according to Dr. Milgram, has failed internationally.

These math methods call for students to draw pictures, complete with circles, hash marks and dots, to compute their answers. The assignments, when completed by young elementary students, often resemble Neanderthal wall drawings, earning the name Caveman Math. For instance, this standard for 4th grade math:

CCSS.MATH.CONTENT.4.OA.A.2
Multiply or divide to solve word problems involving multiplicative comparison, *e.g.*, by using drawings and equations with a symbol for the unknown number to represent the problem, distinguishing multiplicative comparison from additive comparison.

Results in this:

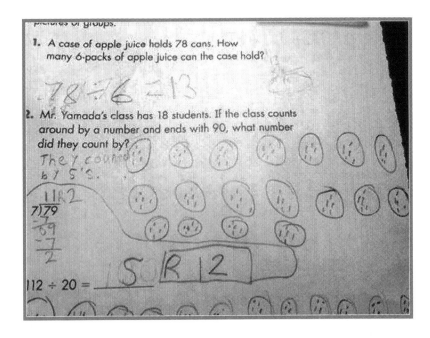

Where did Caveman Math Originate?

The not-so-new new reform math standards, introduced in 1989, are compliments of the National Council of Teachers of Mathematics (NCTM). The NCTM is a group of reformers who have tried selling this type of math at least twice before, revising their standards in 2000 and again in 2006 with what they named *Focal Points*. The standards failed miserably all three times. The standards and supporting curricula were criticized for not using standard algorithms and putting emphasis on non-traditional arithmetic methods.

The American Institutes for Research (AIR) reported in 2005 that the NCTM proposals "risk exposing students to unrealistically advanced mathematics content in the early grades."[73]

A few examples of the reform-supporting curricula introduced in response to the 1989 NCTM standards include:

- Investigations in Numbers, Data, and Space
- Connected Mathematics and
- Everyday math

Today some common supporting curricula includes TERC Investigations, Eureka and Go! Math. Constructivist methods do not offer much in the way of explanation and (recently) don't even offer a textbook. They are extremely time-consuming and parents who didn't learn these controversial methods are rendered helpless during homework time. It does not matter what book a school purchases, if it is aligned to Common Core, it will use the same methods.

Constructivism is based on emotional and self directed learning. The United Nations encourages these methods for its UNESCO members as a means of teaching peace and social equity in the 2005 Teacher Education Frameworks exclaiming, "Constructivism provides the methodology for achieving high-quality instructional processes in education."[74]

The G.W. Bush administration even established a National Math Advisory Panel, who noted in 2008 that there is "no basis in research for preferring one or the other." Further, the final report insists, "Debates regarding the relative importance of conceptual knowledge, procedural skills (*e.g.*, the standard algorithms), and the commitment of addition, subtraction, multiplication, and division facts to long-term memory are misguided. These capabilities are mutually supportive, each facilitating learning of the others. Conceptual understanding of mathematical operations, fluent execution of procedures, and fast access to number combinations together support effective and efficient problem solving." In other words, standard algorithm is necessary and our kids need quick recall of memorized facts to succeed later on.[75]

The standards created by the NCTM were used by many schools as part of the assessment process under No Child Left Behind. Children's math scores did not change or improve, despite NCTM's attempts to mainstream these standards. But they're back again—this time the NCTM piggybacked it onto the Common Core Standards Initiative, with funding from the Bill and Melinda Gates Foundation to make it more sustainable, as Marc Tucker would say. Whenever Mr. or Ms. Common Core try to argue that there is no constructivist math in the Common Core standards, I point out that Professor Jon Star from Harvard is studying the effect of constructivism in the Common Core now, along with Vanderbilt University and the National Science Foundation, which has been pushing reform math since the 1990s. [76]

James Shuls, education policy analyst at the Show-Me Institute, argues, "The bottom line is that the Common Core State Standards are built on constructivist principles and are being implemented, by and large, by constructivist means. If supporters like constructivism, which I suspect most do, then they should just come out and say so. That is not such a difficult position to defend. But don't attempt to tell me these standards won't tell teachers how to teach." [77]

Educator and author Bridgette Wallis remembers, "watching 5th grade [students] 'deep thinking' and 'applying' their math prowess in multiple step word problems... All was fine until they all had to stop their problem and higher-level thinking to put their pencils down and count on their fingers! Deep thinking cannot get very deep when students are stuck on the easiest part. This is constructivist math, it has not changed. Now we have Common Core. Common Core is constructivism tied in a pretty bow and repackaged as math that has not been reformed." [78]

When in doubt, just ask the authors of the standards, Achieve. When comparing NCTM's math standards to Common Core, Achieve notes, "The CCSS are similarly rigorous to NCTM's *Focal Points*. While some content occurs earlier in the CCSS, the two documents *generally describe the same content.*"[79]

Common Core constructivism also calls for arguments and collective reasoning that teaches the "group answer" is right, even when it is wrong. What is this, a game show or a classroom? As adults, they won't be able to draw little stick people or circles with hash marks to answer financial questions in a board meeting, nor will they be able to phone a friend or poll the audience for an answer to an important question that only a leader can make in a moment of crisis.

To make matters worse, constructivism also embodies emphasizing the process used to get the answer, rather than emphasizing the correct answer itself. (This is also evident in the ELA [literacy] standards.) In other words, often the grading is such that $2 + 2=5$ as long as they used the proper abstract method and can argue or demonstrate their answer.

This part of constructivism infuriates me the most. I watched, in horror, a video of a CCSS teacher education workshop online, where corporate sponsored speakers instructed teachers to overlook the answer if it was wrong. See the standards description on the next page for an example of constructivist language:

CCSS.Math.Practice.MP3

Standards for Mathematical Practice » Construct viable arguments and critique the reasoning of others.

Mathematically proficient students understand and use stated assumptions, definitions, and previously established results in constructing arguments. They make conjectures and build a logical progression of statements to explore the truth of their conjectures. They are able to analyze situations by breaking them into cases, and can recognize and use counterexamples. They justify their conclusions, communicate them to others, and respond to the arguments of others. They reason inductively about data, making plausible arguments that take into account the context from which the data arose. Mathematically proficient students are also able to compare the effectiveness of two plausible arguments, distinguish correct logic or reasoning from that which is flawed, and—if there is a flaw in an argument—explain what it is. Elementary students can construct arguments using concrete referents such as objects, drawings, diagrams, and actions. Such arguments can make sense and be correct, even though they are not generalized or made formal until later grades. Later, students learn to determine domains to which an argument applies. Students at all grades can listen or read the arguments of others, decide whether they make sense, and ask useful questions to clarify or improve the arguments.

Honestly. 2 + 2 will always = 4. Math is a law. It doesn't really matter how you *feel* about it. Is *1984* still required reading in high school?

Why is My Child Crying About it?

When parents around the country voice their concerns about the visceral reactions of our children to these methods, as usual we are met with condescending assumptions and remarks implying that we are coddling our children.

We are sarcastically asked if we question the "rigor" in the new standards and then we're accused of not wanting our children to be pushed or challenged. We're told they must have behavior problems or perhaps we should have them tested for Attention Deficit Disorder.

The reason these methods have failed in the past is largely because they conflict with normal cognitive development. Clinical psychologists state that abstract processing does not work for elementary age children because they are in the concrete phase of their development. Elementary children simply are not "wired" for this kind of processing. That explains why my child, and so many others, had such a visceral response to his homework.

Early childhood development professionals were not on the validation committee of the Common Core State Standards Initiative. As a result, elementary school children under the Common Core are suffering physical and emotional responses such as new behavior problems, stress, anxiety and depression.

In 2010, the Alliance for Childhood issued a statement, signed by 500 early childhood professionals, declaring that the standards, "conflict with compelling new research in cognitive science, neuroscience, child development, and early childhood education about how young children learn, what they need to learn, and how best to teach them in kindergarten and the early grades." Since then, Dr. Carla Horowitz of the Yale Child Study Center states, "The Core Standards will cause suffering, not learning, for many, many young children."[80]

CCSS Mathematical Practices:
2. Reason abstractly and quantitatively - repeated in every grade level
3. Construct viable arguments and critique the reasoning of others.
K-12 Standards for Mathematical Practice »
Reason abstractly and quantitatively. Mathematically proficient students make sense of quantities and their relationships in problem situations. They bring two complementary abilities to bear on problems involving quantitative relationships: the ability to decontextualize— to abstract a given situation

---

Dr. Gary Thompson is a Doctor of Clinical Psychology. He is the Director of Clinical Training and Community Advocacy in private practice in Utah. This father of four public school children calls the constructivism in the CCSS, "Cognitive Child Abuse."[81] Our early childhood development experts were not given a voice.

ASSURANCE #1/PART 2: THE ASSESSMENTS

"Not everything that counts can be counted, and not everything that can be counted counts." - Albert Einstein

The second part of Secretary Duncan's Assurance #1 is common assessments. When we applied for the Race to the Top money, we agreed not only to adopt common standards, but also to utilize new next generation assessment tools designed to complement those standards. Test consortiums have been established for this purpose. A test consortium is a group of states that joined with the contracted Pearson Education to develop new state-of-the-art computer-based tests. States must pay to belong to the consortiums. For instance, my state pays $250,000 per year to be a member of one of them.

PARCC AND SBAC/AIR

The two consortiums are PARCC, the Partnership for the Assessment of Readiness for College and Careers and the Smarter Balanced Assessment Consortium (SBAC), which has recently partnered with the American Institutes for Research (AIR). These consortiums received a combined total of $360 million from the federal government, even though "the federal government has nothing to do with Common Core."

AIR is not a state consortium. It is actually a research organization specializing in *non-cognitive and behavioral research*. AIR is funded by George Soros's open society organization and recently put down roots in Washington D.C.

This slide, which is posted for public viewing at https://sites.google.com/site/cteccss/, ties together everything the proponents don't want us paying attention to: The new language that our teachers must speak, the connection of the standards to the testing and data collection, the federal funding and the new subject matter coming down the pike. Words like sea change, mandates, common language, tested and measured, more subject areas send a clear message about who is charge and what the agenda is.

This says a lot about their perspective on this reform. This presentation provides recommendations for integrating the CCSS into Career and Technical Education, or CTE. It tells teachers how to fold the CCSS into curriculum, instruction and assessment. This is despite the fact that Mr. and Ms. Common Core say that curriculum has nothing to do with Common Core. I digress...

What's the big deal?

* The CCSS initiative is a "sea change" in education for teaching and learning!
* The CCSS mandates the student learning outcomes for every grade level.
* The CCSS force a common language. Your staff will begin using this language.
* Students will be tested and instructional effectiveness will be measured based on CCSS.
* Federal funding is tied to CCSS adoption, implementation, and accountability.
* English Language Arts and Mathematics CCSS are just the beginning. . more subject area standards are being developed.

 AIR

Previously, we measured student achievement in my home state of Arkansas by using the norm-referenced Iowa Test of Basic Skills (ITBS) every spring. The ITBS was completed on paper and had a fixed cost.

Now PARCC will replace the ITBS for grades 3 and above. And the rules have changed.

Lack of Transparency

The law regarding test transparency was changed, relieving PARCC of any responsibility of providing parents with an idea of what their students will read when they sit for the test, compared to 50% transparency with the ITBS. Furthermore, the cost is not fixed. As states leave the consortium, and so far 11 have, the cost of the test rises.

Norm-Referenced vs. Criterion-Referenced Tests

Further, as I stated earlier, the ITBS and the new tests differ in what they measure. In an April, 2014 interview I conducted with noted special education expert and advocate Dr. Meg Norris, she stated,

> It is important to note that PARCC and SBAC do not measure the same things as the ITBS achievement tests. PARCC, SBAC and any other state-standardized test is what they call a criterion-referenced test and they measure knowledge of the standards at one single grade level. Period. The others, like the Iowa, are norm-referenced tests and they measure academic ability at multiple levels and compare students across grade levels. It identifies the level of achievement. Norm referenced tests are the best measurements and generally give teachers better information.

Higher Costs

In addition to membership fees and fluctuating testing costs, these new computer-based assessments require Internet bandwidth and hardware that many of our schools lack. So of course, the Common Core profiteers and the state departments of education are begging their legislatures for funding, relating sob stories of how our children are suffering in school without Internet access.

Every Common Core state is being convinced that they are somehow behind everyone else because their schools are technologically backward without sufficient bandwidth. The reality is that we would not be discussing the need for expanding bandwidth if it weren't for PARCC and SBAC. This is purely back door funding for their assessment methodology and therefore part of the overall, outrageous burden of cost the states must bear for CCSS implementation.

The states will probably pay much more to implement the assessments associated with the Common Core standards than is available from the federal money we were given. And in Arkansas, the assessment itself is meaningless with no previous benchmark for comparison. So what are we spending all this money on? What are we getting for our investment? How do we know the standards are really working?

TEST FLAWS

The state of New York and a handful of others are ahead of Arkansas in implementation by 2 years. They are reporting numerous flaws with the tests including:

- Cultural and regional flaws in the wording (*e.g.*, moccasin the shoe vs. Moccasin the snake)
- Cognitively inappropriate, complicated test questions/test questions worded at a grade level higher than the student
- Product placement

- Severe testing anxiety in students
- Lack of typing/computer skills for underprivileged children resulting in low scores, widening the achievement gap

NATIONAL EXAMS AFFECTED: GED, ACT AND SAT

Most of the national exams have been affected by this reform as well. Many argue that it is too early in the implementation process to make such drastic changes. But hey, they have profits to make! For instance, our good friends in London at Pearson Education purchased our General Education Development (GED) exam, aligned it to the Common Core standards and tripled the price.

ACT, Inc. is a corporate partner in this reform and as part of the workforce-steering effort, ACT offers a triple threat for workforce development: the three tests comprising the "The Educational Planning and Assessment System (EPAS) Workforce Pathways Assessment." [82]Testing begins with *Aspire* in 8th and again 10th grade. Then, in the 11th grade, the ACT is administered, as usual.

Of course, the ACT test itself is already aligned to Common Core standards.[83] Questions are being added to reflect the Common Core's emphasis on tracing ideas through multiple texts and its increased focus on statistics. The ACT will also contain optional open-ended questions to assess students' ability to explain and support their claims, making grading more subjective.

The SAT is owned by the College Board, another corporate partner of the CCSSI. Remember David Coleman from Achieve and Student Achievement Partners? He is now the president of the College Board. Crony Capitalism strikes again! He plans to align the SAT to CCSSI in

2016.[84] The College Board also owns the Advanced Placement (AP) program, which allows students to take college-level courses and exams and earn college credit or placement while still in high school.

While the ACT only needed minor modifications to align to the Common Core, the SAT required an overhaul. The amount of time allotted per question was increased up to 49%, the ELA sections are now almost identical to the ACT and the math section is chock-full of constructivism. Test expert Jed Applerouth found, "This minor rewording is indicative of just how deeply the new Math section is tied to the Common Core. The new SAT Math questions drive right through the heart of Common Core by relying less upon heuristic problem solving (*i.e.*, when you see this kind of problem, employ this strategy) and more upon conceptual understanding of math principles."[85]

Applerouth also asserts, "The redesigned SAT is effectively a 12th-grade Common Core assessment designed to rival the forthcoming tests from PARCC and Smarter Balanced, consortiums tasked by the Department of Education with developing the Common Core tests for the 21st century. And this redesigned SAT is just the first step: The College Board explicitly revealed plans to release similar Common-Core tests for every grade level, from middle school to high school."

Will the traditional college entrance exams survive Common Core? Or will they fade to black like a rotten apple core?

Chapter

8

Assurance #2: Unreasonable Search and Seizure

"It is time to prepare every child, everywhere in America,
to out-compete any worker, anywhere in the world. It is time to give all
Americans a complete and competitive education
from the cradle up through a career."
~ President Barack Obama

Secretary Duncan's Assurance #2 calls for State Longitudinal Data Systems. While data mining in education is not new, data mining by the federal government and private corporations at the *individual* student level *is* new.

In 1988, The National Center for Education Statistics compiled a report called Youth Indicators. It analyzed data concerning the student's family, health, economics, social and extracurricular activity as it related to education. Not only were students surveyed, but the report also pulled data from the Department of Health and Human Services, The Department of Labor and the Department of Commerce.[86]

In addition, a report by the Department of Education called *Enhancing Data Mining and Learning Analytics* is worth reading. In this report, parents can learn how our children's mouse clicks have been mined for years in the name of improving education.[87] These data mining initiatives were conducted rather anonymously and the results were not tied to a student record. Data collection in education has now changed.

STATE LONGITUDINAL DATABASE SYSTEM (SLDS)

Essentially, the U.S. DOE would like an easier way to drill down to student-level data that is all in one place. The Second Assurance addresses this desire with the State Longitudinal Database Systems (SLDS), using the P-20 data collection model.

A "VIRTUAL" NATIONAL DATABASE

It is against the law for the United States Department of Education to have a national student database. Instead, in 2002, a law was passed that gave the federal government permission to provide a template to the states to create their own state longitudinal database systems. These State Longitudinal Databases can now be linked up and voila! we have a *de facto* national database. I guess you don't have to break the law when you can find such a simple way to *bend* it.

The states can choose from two models: The National Education Data Model (NEDM) or the Common Education Data Standards (CEDS). Each list has over 400 data elements to collect on students, their families, teachers and schools. I encourage parents to download the list. Arkansas adopted the NEDM; your state may have chosen the CEDS. Either way, you can export the long list to a spreadsheet to view it.

What's Collected

The data elements are posted for public comment. Fortunately, some of the most offensive data elements have been removed from newer versions due to public outcry. Be sure to find out which version your state is using as some of those offensive fields may be in use for your state under a former version (2.0, 3.0, 4.0 etc.)

The data collection includes non-cognitive behavioral profiles and test scores and it is based on workforce-steering, much like the German system of education and Tucker's model. Companies like Pearson and ACT feel they know what is best for your child. To heck with the American dream. Instead of asking, "What would you like to be when you grow up?" we can start asking, "Who would you like to work for when you grow up?"

The Connection to Common Core

So what is the connection to Common Core? The owners of the standards, the Council of Chief State School Officers (CCSSO) tout a *"Continued Commitment to Disaggregation"* in their mission statement. The CCSSO has established the Education Information Management Advisory Consortium (EIMAC) to collect and report data, design and manage information systems and to "reduce the burden of data collection" at the national level—*in other words, to place the burden of national data collection on the states.*[88]

The CCSS initiative also partnered with several private and public agencies for data collection and sharing. For example, one is called the Data Quality Campaign and they state: "As states build and enhance K12 longitudinal data systems they continue building *linkages* to exchange and use information across early childhood postsecondary and the *work-*

force and with other critical agencies such as *health, social services, and criminal justice systems.* "[89] (Emphasis added.)

Here's what The US Department of Education has to say about their grant-money-for-data programs, just in case anyone wants to argue that the federal government has nothing to do with it, or that this data collection has nothing to do with Common Core:

> ...the Recovery Act [ARRA] (insert: State Fiscal Stabilization Funds) requires that Race to the Top funds be awarded to States that have made significant progress in establishing such longitudinal data systems and in meeting other performance objectives related to higher standards and better assessments, teacher effectiveness and equity in teacher distribution, and supporting and turning around low performing schools.[90]

Our Children and Workforce Management

The Department of Labor wants that information so they can manage the economy. The Workforce Data Quality Initiative and SLDS goal for States is to use these longitudinal data systems to *"follow individuals through school and into and through their work life."*[91] (Emphasis added.) [92] The Department of Labor even gave Arkansas $18 million in Federal funds to support this data initiative. How much did your state get? Find out at this site: http://nces.ed.gov/programs/slds/state.asp.

Fellow *Arkansas Against Common Core* Board member and high school student Pat Richardson points out that CEOs of big corporate data companies refer to this as "open data," as if student information is public property and theirs for the taking. In the past, student data has always been collected and reported on in an *aggregated*, very anonymous basis and did not go beyond state lines.

There was an event at the White House in the summer of 2012 called Education Datapalooza, where CEOs from big data companies got together to brag about how they planned to use our students' data to further these education reforms. The CEO of eScholar, Shawn Bay, was quick to refer to the Common Core State Standards as the "glue that actually ties everything together."[93] If all the students are not using the same standards and taking the same tests, then the big data guns say they are comparing apples to oranges. Now that everyone is playing by the same rules, they can compare apples to apples. The big data companies need the CCSS to make their profits and products work. This allows them to profit off our tax dollars and violate our privacy at the same time! How convenient for them.

The Memorandum of Understanding

In addition to agreeing to this data initiative by applying for Race to the Top, states that agree to use the standardized tests associated with Common Core (PARCC or SBAC) sign an agreement that requires them to share data. So, if you only read the standards, you won't see anything about data mining. The federal mandate for data is in the testing consortiums agreement, commonly referred to as the PARCC or SBAC *Memorandum of Understanding* (MOU).

Excerpts of the contract are below:

"6) The Grantee must provide timely and complete access to any and all data collected at the State level to ED or its designated program monitors, technical assistance providers, or research partners, and to GAO, and the auditors conducting the audit required by 34 CFR section 80.26."[94]

"b) Producing all student-level data in a manner consistent with an industry-recognized open-licensed interoperability standards that is approved by the Department during the grant period."[95]

This means that the consortium (not the individual state's department of education) and its hired vendor, has the data and is required to provide the federal government and others education "researchers" with access to the data. Under this arrangement, multinational organizations such as Micrsoft, Cisco, Intel, Pearson, AIR, Google and many others, now meet the definition of a researcher or partner. The state has very little control over the data or where it goes once it is in the SLDS.

THE FAMILY EDUCATION RIGHT TO PRIVACY ACT. ADIOS.

The state department of education will say that they have always collected and reported data on students and that we are protected by FERPA. They fail to understand two things: the data is not in their possession to share and FERPA was relaxed.

What's a FERPA, you ask?

The Family Education Right to Privacy Act. It is supposed to protect student data. However, in preparation for this initiative, in 2011, the United States Department of Education, with a pen and a phone, gutted the regulatory pieces of this law by removing the requirement for parental consent. Section 99.7(a) was changed to say that they *no longer need parental consent* to gather or share this data.[96] We are no longer protected by FERPA; now education entities can collect and share any type of student data without a parent's knowledge or consent.

Remember, per the testing consortium contract, the student data resides in an SLDS that can be accessed by private agencies and the federal government. The state department of education doesn't have to *share* it. The proponents are correct when they say that there is nothing in the Common Core State Standards pertaining to data collection.

It's not in the standards. Common Core is more than standards. It's in the testing agreement. It's not that the state is going to *willingly* share the data with the federal government and all its corporate cronies; rather the federal government and multinational corporations will access it on their own. The United States government, including the Department of Labor, Health and Human Services, the Criminal Justice System and hundreds of private corporations and non-profit agencies can now collect, share, buy and sell over 400 elements of your child's personal data without your knowledge or your consent.

Can we sue for this?

The Electronic Privacy Information Center (EPIC) filed a lawsuit over this data initiative but the case was dismissed due to lack of standing. A student's rights must be violated *with consequences* before a lawsuit can be an effective tool against this invasion of privacy.

While this experiment moves forward, we're supposed to wait until a student is denied the school or job of their choice due to someone's interpretation of the data or until a security breach yields personal information to the public domain. Not only will the federal government have detailed information on its citizenry, corporations will have loads of marketing data for their advertising campaigns and The Department of Labor can start driving the fulfillment of workforce needs.

In the meantime, the bill mill ALEC was quick to offer sample legislation for the states to use as a means of protection.[97] To date, while other states are passing privacy laws in reaction to Common Core, only Oklahoma has used this particular template.

In response to recent public outcry, the CCSSO published a letter about Common Core data in attempt to quell parent concerns. Several state anti-Common Core coalitions published a fiery response. You can read both letters at the link shown below. *Arkansas Against Common Core* proudly contributed to the response.

Open Letter and response from coalitions: http://edlibertywatch.org/category/data-collection-and-data-privacy.

Biometric Data

Another change to FERPA includes the definition of Personally Identifiable Information which now is expanded to include: "Biometric Record," which encompasses, "Biological or behavioral characteristics including fingerprints, retina and iris patterns, voiceprints, DNA Sequence, Facial Characteristics, and handwriting" (Authority 20 USC, 1232g.).[98]

What on earth do these biometrics, including facial expressions and DNA sequences, have to do with education? Why do they need this information?

It Can Happen Here—Today

I'm reading the new regulatory changes the U.S. DOE made to the Family Education Right to Privacy Act (FERPA). In the company of my 5th grade daughter, I comment aloud on biometrics being added to the act's definition of personally identifiable information, wondering about the purpose of such data in education circles. My daughter replies that she's been using her fingerprint to check out books from the library at school since last year.

For a moment, I am struck breathless. Certainly, in the stack of forms we completed at the beginning of the school year, I must have signed something giving permission for this. I must have just missed the fine print. Or, perhaps I mistakenly threw away a note that was sent home. Nope. As I continue reading about the changes to FERPA, I realize the school didn't need permission.

As of 2012, parental consent is no longer required to collect or share personally identifiable information. Some Internet searches reveal that other parents are reporting iris scans for bus transportation and fingerprint scanners in the cafeterias. I continue feeling like the wind has been knocked out of me.

I make an appointment with the principal and the librarian at our elementary school to discuss the fact that they are using my children's fingerprints. They are very helpful and kind and share information from the software vendor's web page with me.

I even get a demonstration of the software and assurance that the system does not store my daughter's fingerprint. It deletes the fingerprint, they tell me, and keeps only a "template." They say this system is something the school has been trying to obtain for some time and relate their excitement at getting it last year. The fingerprint scanner makes the checkout process faster, and they no longer have to worry about kids losing their cards. No, they never requested a signed consent form, and they never sent a note to parents advising them their child's fingerprint would be used.

I am still disturbed. There is a lack of consistency here. If my child wishes to go on a field trip, I have to sign a permission slip. I have to sign a photo release for any school-related pictures of my children to be used and a release for my children to be listed in the school directory. But no consent is needed for fingerprints?

If my friend wishes to serve as a substitute teacher at our school, she must be fingerprinted and sign a consent allowing that along with a background check. Yet, my children were fingerprinted without my knowledge or consent.

No Security Risk?

I return home and research the information the school has provided. The technology vendor, identiMetrics, explains that the fingerprint itself is not stored; rather a template is created forming a binary number. That binary number is assigned to the student's bar code and ID number. Therefore, according to the vendor, and other proponents of biometric fingerprint scanning, no security risk is posed and the child's identity cannot be hacked.

identiMetrics boasts that "Once the students are enrolled in the identiMetrics Finger Scanning ID System, they can be identified quickly and accurately to another third party software application that uses swipe card, bar code, or ID number input."[99]

The template itself is individually identifiable to the student. As identiMetrics says, this binary code can be used to rapidly link different databases and create a profile without consent. Further, according to *The U.S. Government National Science and Technology Council*, a user can reconstruct a fingerprint image from the template and government security experts have *successfully hacked* the fingerprint scanners used in schools.[100]

Kim Cameron, the chief architect of Access in Microsoft's™ Connected Systems Division, and creator of The 7 Laws of Identity, disagrees with using this technology in schools when he advises, "If you want to find out who owns a fingerprint, just convert the fingerprint to a template and do a search for the template in one of these databases. Call the template a binary number if you want to. The point is that all you need to save in the database is the number. Later, when you come across a 'fingerprint of interest' you just convert it to a number and search for it. Law enforcement can use this information—and so can criminals."[101]

The National Academy of Sciences has released a report entitled *"Biometric Recognition: Challenges and Opportunities."* The report concluded that biometric recognition technologies are "inherently probabilistic and hence inherently fallible." [102] The Electronic Privacy Information Center (EPIC) says, "sources of uncertainty in biometric systems include variation within persons, sensors, feature extraction and matching algorithms, and data integrity."[103]

Some states have banned the use of this technology in schools and others have enacted legislation that requires parental consent. Biometric scanning is opposed by the *American Civil Liberties Union of Florida* and the *Electronic Privacy Information Center.* School districts in cities including Boulder, Colorado, and Irvine, California, have rejected fingerprint-scanning programs as well. The United Kingdom has already been down this road and since made the decision to ban the biometric scanning without parental consent.

The aforementioned biometrics vendor, identiMetrics, has partnered with none other than Pearson Education! Pearson also has software agreements with more than 50 other vendors, many of whom fit the loose definition of "Agency" in FERPA.

Why was DNA Sequence added to FERPA?

The *Newborn Screening Saves Lives Reauthorization Act* was passed this year (2014) extending the grant for five more years. This law mandates newborn bloodspot screenings and provides grant money for the management of the resulting data. Unbeknownst to most moms, those bloodspots provide DNA sequence information and are stored in a national clearinghouse for genetic research. Some states collect the DNA information and some do not.

As part of their Race to the Top Proposal, and the Early Learning Challenge program, Rhode Island committed to merging their State Longitudinal Database System (SDLS) with the state health clinical information system, thereby storing *individual* infant DNA sequence information as part of the student record, which—let me remind you—is no longer protected under FERPA. The proposal reads, "Rhode Island's proposed early learning data system will be linked to both the state's K-12 data system and to the state's universal newborn screening and health data system, helping to identify children with high needs, track participation in programs and track children's development and learning."[104]

From the cradle to the grave....

WHAT'S THE BIG DEAL? THERE IS NO SUCH THING AS PRIVACY ANYMORE.

It is logical to assume that like any other data collected, biometric data, personally identifiable information tied directly to the student identification number, could make its way through the data collection and reporting pathway to an unknown number of private corporations and government agencies, without parental consent.

This brings up several issues that need to be addressed. The first obvious risk is a data breach, which has already occurred in New York. For instance, in November of 2013, a 17-year-old was arrested for stealing the data of 15,000 students from 18 schools and plastering it on an external web site. The data was housed in the student data repository InBloom, developed by Rupert Murdoch's team of phone "hijackers," funded by Gates and Carnegie and residing on an Amazon.com cloud server. Thankfully, InBloom announced in 2014 that it is effectively shutting down after states, including New York, withdrew from the agreement.

Unfortunately, because this kind of data collection is mandated by the federal government under this reform, there are already plenty of other companies chomping at the bit to provide this unnecessary service while passing the buck to the state tax payers. As is the case with the standards, the states that withdrew from InBloom, will likely face a "rebrand" in the name of what Barber likes to call, "sustainable, or irreversible reform."

The Bottom Line: This SLDS scheme leads to national, individually identifiable data collection. Aside from losing our privacy, this opens the door to discrimination. Our children may lose opportunities to attend a particular school or to get a job based on someone's interpretation or access to the data. The standards serve to support this data collection—they are symbiotic.

This is a constitutional violation of the Fourth Amendment. The reformers circumvented the system and found a back door to gain access to our children's personal information. The constitution defines our God-given right to privacy: The right of the people to be secure in their persons, houses, papers and effects against unreasonable searches and seizure *shall not be violated*. Except, maybe, by the Common Core State Standards Initiative and the Student Longitudinal Database System.

Chapter

9

Assurance # 3:
Teacher Evaluation Systems

If a doctor, lawyer, or dentist had 40 people in his office at one time,
all of whom had different needs, and some of whom didn't want to be
there and were causing trouble, and the doctor, lawyer, or dentist,
without assistance, had to treat them all with professional excellence
for nine months, then he might have some conception
of the classroom teacher's job.
~ Donald D. Quinn

TEACHER EVALUATIONS

As part of their proposal in the Race to the Top application, states were asked to demonstrate how they planned to implement new state-of-the-art teacher evaluation systems. This single element on the application was worth more points than any other, 138. Part of this system ties the teacher's performance evaluation to how students perform on high-stakes standardized tests, specifically the PARCC or SBAC assessment.

Tests are not a reliable indicator of true academic achievement. As a parent, I disagree that a teacher's evaluation should be based on how their students do on a high-stakes test. Further, these new teacher evaluation systems are steeped in bureaucracy and paperwork. Teachers are now spending more time completing paperwork when they should be spending time in the classroom with our children. Finally, these evaluation systems set unreal expectations. For instance, one sample evaluation form rates the teacher on whether or not the students erupt in a round of applause after a lesson. Give me a break.

TEACHING TO THE TEST

This approach of tying the teacher's evaluation to test scores increases the "teaching to the test" mentality that we so disliked with No Child Left Behind. It completely removes personal responsibility from the student or the family. It embodies a collectivist mentality that somehow expects our teachers to make up for elements outside their control, such as poverty, lack of parental support and the child's personality traits or problems. Again, it means less time teaching and more time preparing for tests and completing paperwork. This will drive our best teachers out of the field. We will lose our veteran teachers and our children will lose time in the classroom to provide "accountability" for federal dollars.

GOOD VS. BAD TEACHERS

As parents, we are tired of hearing legislators repeatedly using the word "accountability" to justify the excessive mega-testing of our kids. Mr. and Ms. Common Core will assert that we clearly do not wish to have "good" teachers and that "bad" teachers are the problem. The reality is that we already know who the good teachers are; we don't need tests and bureaucratic reports to find them. Discussing the good teachers is a common topic among parents—often discussed in social gatherings, at work, at church etc. Parents are always trying to get their kids into the "good" teachers' classrooms. We do not need tests to differentiate between them.

STUDENT REVOLT

Conveniently, Pearson owns the TPA, or the Teacher Performance Assessment tool. In May 2012, students and teachers in the University of Massachusetts, Amherst Campus School of Education resisted with a national campaign challenging the forced implementation of this assessment tool.

They argued that the field supervisors and cooperating teachers who guided their teaching practice, and observed and evaluated them for six months, were better equipped to judge their teaching skills and potential than people who had never seen nor spoken with them. They have refused to participate in a pilot program organized by Pearson and to submit the two 10-minute videos of themselves teaching and a take-home test. This kind of resistance is what it takes to restore local control. It is basic supply and demand. What we allow will continue.

TEACHER TRAINING

This assurance also includes comprehensive teacher retraining. Gates-hired facilitators receive a $5,000 stipend to travel the country and brainwash our teachers into teaching in lockstep with Common Core. He is all about changing teaching because clearly teachers are the problem, right? As I mentioned earlier, I have yet to see a study, or any research, which points to teachers being the problem that plagues our education system. So far, everything I have read points to poverty being the issue and centralized planning won't help that either.

The argument that Common Core allows for teacher flexibility regarding methods and materials is only a half-truth. Teachers can be as flexible as Gates wants them to be. Because of the Common Core, Gates is spending millions paying teachers to attend workshops and to then tell other teachers how to do their jobs. Once again, the majority of those who endorse Common Core have been paid to do so.

Chapter
10

Assurance #4: Bring in the Charters/Close Low-Achieving Schools

"The greatest dangers to liberty lurk in insidious encroachment by men of zeal, well-meaning but without understanding."
[Olmstead v. U.S., 277 U.S. 438 (1928) (dissenting)]
— Louis D. Brandeis

ASSURANCE # 4: ADDRESSING LOW-PERFORMING SCHOOLS

The United States Department of Education loves charter schools, as evidenced by the millions of dollars they are funneling to individual states to create them. States touting plans for charter schools could earn 40 points on their Race to the Top Application and win separate grants later. Every state has a different reform proposal on this topic, ranging from lifting enrollment caps to closing public schools.

Although charter schools are public and free, their enrollment is limited and parents must apply to get their child into a specific school, often through a lottery system. Some charters are independent and non-profit, while others are run by for-profit private corporations. Charters receive government education dollars but operate at the discretion of the district or the state.

EMO CHARTERS: THE ISSUES

At a recent conference in California, the CEO of Netflix, Reed Hastings, bragged about the charter movement. He said that their goal was to have the entire public school system 90% charter-based.[105] As of 2012, about 5.8% of public school students are in a charter school.[106] This begs several questions. Why are we so eager to listen to a corporate CEO about education reform? What does a corporate CEO have to gain from a for-profit charter movement? What's in it for Netflix?

Losing Parental Input

The charter movement began with schools that were started by communities and parent-led. Corporations seized a market opportunity and now we have charters run by Education Management Organizations (EMOs). Charters run by EMOs, as opposed to community-led charters, present a slippery slope for parents. Traditionally, most parents have seen charter schools as a great thing, and many are. EMO charters, however, are a multi-billion dollar market. One of the unexpected consequences to this reform is that the massive expansion of charters ushers in some realities that many parents (and teachers) are starting to question. EMO Charters are not accountable for the spending of our tax dollars. Unless you reside in a "local district" state, there is often no local elected board attached to a charter.

So, assuming that Hastings gets his wish, and 90% of our public schools are replaced with EMO charters, when the next federal reform comes down the pike, where will parents turn to make their voices heard? On the positive side, if the parent doesn't like the school, they can simply apply to another one without fighting the bureaucracy of school boards and zoning rules. What happens when your child is not chosen in the enrollment lottery?

CIVIL RIGHTS ISSUES

The latest massive EMO charter experiment is taking place in New Orleans, where an entire district was shut down and *every* public school was converted to a charter. The true crisis that ushered in this change was Hurricane Katrina. In this case, the charters are not paying rent. The tax-payer-funded buildings were *given* to the profit-generating charters. The other interesting consequence is that the Orleans Parish School Board fired more than 7,000 employees, most of them African Americans. They couldn't find work because the private charters chose to hire young *Teach for America* facilitators, most of whom, of course, were white. The fired teachers sued and won.

Teachers are not the only ones claiming that charters are "the new segregation." Communities all over the country are reporting that charters are favoring enrollment for high-performing white students who provide the test scores needed to keep the charters open, and that low-performing students are asked to leave. Citizens in Detroit and Newark have filed civil rights complaints.[107]

There are good charters and bad charters. For instance, in Washington DC this year, eight charters have applied for approval. One of the scarier proposals is an Arabic immersion school that touts using the U.N. model of education. Another charter wants approval for two middle schools that focus on international education (there's the U.N. again!). However, there were also encouraging proposals for a K-8 school that focuses on special education and another for adults that serves drop-outs with education and job placement assistance.[108]

SUMMARY OF ISSUES

Following are some of the issues facing parents with the increase in charter schools, especially EMO charters:

- How do we make our voices heard and influence policy with a private group, which, very often, is from another state?

- How do we ensure we have representation regarding the spending of our tax dollars? They are not accountable to anyone.

- Who determines what makes a good charter versus a bad charter? Who decides?

- What happens when the public school has been closed and you end up with a bad charter? What happens when a bad charter closes and leaves after the public school was closed?

- What are parents to do when a charter expels their child for low academic achievement?

- Is it fair that some students ride or drive more than two hours in rural areas to attend a charter because their public school was closed in its favor?

This part of education reform may create a better learning environment in the short term, but EMO charters sacrifice the liberty of the parents' voice in education, leaving us without representation. Couple this with state laws that isolate parents and consolidate local schools and we have a looming disaster, especially for students in rural and poverty-stricken areas. Parents need to be involved and vigilant with decisions moving forward. They need to be alert and wary of the ever-increasing role of public-private partnerships in K-12 education and demand education with representation.

Chapter
11

The Bully Bandwagon

Ridicule is man's most potent weapon.
~ Saul Alinsky, Rules for Radicals

Be careful when questioning where the reformers are taking us. You'll be labeled a tinfoil-hat-wearing conspiracy theorist who chases black helicopters in your minivan! So far, I've been called paranoid, Henny Penny (The sky is falling!), a right-wing conspiracy theorist whack-job, a helicopter parent, a tea party crazy (even though I am not a member of the tea party and have voted both Democratic and Republican in recent elections), a public school hater and a grandstanding idiot. But what's in a name?

Since all the proponents of CCSSI use the same playbook from the U.S. Chamber of Commerce, the NGA or New Venture, they employ the same propaganda messages. For instance, parents across state lines have all been called conspiracy theorists, right-wing extremists and fear-mongers. We've all been accused of preferring the previous "lower" standards in our state and of not wanting our kids to be able to compete in the "21st Century Global Economy." The list goes on with logical fallacies.

WHERE WERE "THESE PEOPLE?"

One common battle cry from the lovers of Common Core is, "Where were *these people* four years ago? Concerned parents are now "these people?" I beg your pardon, speaking to the elected and appointed bureaucrats asking the question. As the person who pays your salary, and as it is so often *condescendingly* quoted to me when I question the Common Core's efficacy, "Please allow me to share some information with you about the Common Core."

"We gave it the benefit of the doubt and didn't know much about it until last year *because there was an implementation timeline." That's* where we were. In the dark and pummeled with propaganda. See below:

- 13.02.2 The following timeline will lead to full implementation of the Common Core State Standards *during the 2013-2014* school year: (Emphasis added.)
- 13.02.2.1 Grades K-2 2011-2012 school year
- 13.02.2.2 Grades 3-8 2012-2013 school year
- 13.02.2.3 Grades 9-12 2013-2014 school year

As you see, Mr./Ms. Common Core, parents weren't involved in the development or implementation and all we had to go on was the propaganda. Now that this reform has hit our kitchen tables in the form of homework, and we see it first hand, we are expressing our concerns. You see, four years ago, we trusted you. Weren't we silly?

BI-PARTISAN OPPOSITION

Another popular distraction is the assertion that only right-wing conservatives are opposed to Common Core. Truthfully, both parties can agree on this one issue. The Republican National Committee *did* make opposition to Common Core part of the party platform in 2013 and the Tea party was one of the first groups to call attention to the issue. Conservative organizations such as The CATO Institute, The Heritage Foundation, The Pioneer Institute and the American Principles Project openly oppose Common Core.

However, Democrats are fighting back as well. A Democratic caucus in Seattle unanimously opposed Common Core in a resolution in 2013 and a coalition called Democrats Against Common Core has taken root. United Opt Out National is a progressive liberal coalition that is opposed to Common Core and the standardized testing culture. The liberal-leaning Badass Teachers Association, led by a progressive liberal educator, opposes Common Core.

This is not a party-line issue. In fact, a book has been released called, *Common Ground on Common Core*, which presents essays from both sides of the political spectrum against Common Core. And despite Mr. and Ms. Common Core accusing parents of "being political" we all know that as long as it is funded with tax dollars, education has always been and will always be a political issue.

RIDICULE

The tactics of ridicule are used often by some proponents of Common Core in an attempt to discredit the opposition. In this case, we are 1) crazy or 2) late to the party and thus missed our chance. Either way, we should be seen in the carpool line and not heard. Apparently, my job as a parent is to do what the State asks me to do. Get the kids to school on time and the state will take care of the rest, because after all, they know better.

Representative Lair's
tin foil-covered desk

Take member of the Bully Bandwagon of Educrats (BBE), Representative Lair in Missouri for example. In response to parents asking for repeal of the CCSSI in his state, he arrogantly added an amendment for tinfoil to the budget. No, he didn't joke about it, he actually did it. The language of the amendment called for *"two rolls of high density aluminum to create headgear designed to deflect drone and/or black helicopter mind-reading and control technology."*[109] They should add a line item for Kool-Aid to the budget and call for him to resign for incompetence. Alas, for him, the Missouri House did even better. First, they covered his entire desk in tin foil. Then two months later, they repealed Common Core in Missouri.

Just a few months after Arizona withdrew from their Common Core testing consortium, another member of the BBE, Arizona School Superintendent John Huppenthal, referred to opponents of the Common Core State Standards as "barbarians at the gate." He went on to say that in his support of the CCSSI, "I put my career on the line to stave off the barbarians."[110] This kind of disrespectful culture trickles down. Another member of the Arizona Department of Education refers to a teacher who spoke out against Common Core, as a "F*cktard."[111] Fortunately, the superintendent position in Arizona is elected, and in the election several weeks later, the barbarians voted him out by over 66,000 votes.[112]

PAID HECKLERS?

Here in Arkansas, our coalition, *Arkansas Against Common Core*, decided to have a rally at the capital before the fiscal legislative session began. On a rainy day, we had a good turnout for our first rally, with just over 120 people. The day before the event a woman, a stranger to me, went on Facebook and launched a counter protest accusing me of spreading misinformation. She showed up with a band of four cronies with their own signs. Both groups were cordial and went about the rally. Then, during my speech, I was heckled by a woman in the audience, not just once but three times. It turns out this counter-protest was organized by someone working for a prominent PR organization that represents the state department of education. The heckler is an attorney with the Arkansas Department of Education.

The Bully Bandwagon of Educrats just keeps rolling on, trying to flatten all opposition. You have to grow a thick skin to bear up under all the insults that will be hurled your way if you take up the cause against the Common Core. Or just a sense of humor. Maybe you could make yourself one of those tinfoil hats.

Chapter

12

The Propaganda Machine: Gallup to the Gallows

"By the skillful and sustained use of propaganda, one can make a people see even heaven as hell or an extremely wretched life as paradise."
~ Adolf Hitler

CLASS SIZE VS. CLASS SIZE

One popular topic of discussion in our education system is about class size. What is the proper number of children in a classroom? This single element often drives parents to turn to home school or private or charter schools, because we all know that a properly managed class size benefits student achievement—smaller is better. The proponents of the CCSS initiative have a different concept of class size.

They like their own class size to be very small. Their class is the elite, filled with corporate bureaucrats who think they're smarter and know better (about everything) than everyone else does. Their small class allows them to stay in power and continue making profits while the larger, managed "economy" class stays in line and does what they are told.

PUBLIC OPINION OF THE COMMON CORE

In April of 2014, a Gallup poll conducted on public opinion regarding the Common Core State Standards Initiative was released. It found that 61% of public school parents had no opinion of or had not heard of it.[113] That tells you just how "state-led" this initiative really wasn't.

The rich elitists pushing this reform have invested millions in private marketing and public relations support. They even have a playbook called the *Common Core Communications Toolkit,* with funding from familiar sources like Gates, New Venture, Carnegie, Achieve, Harvard and the U.S. Chamber of Commerce. The media spin seeks to create a crisis or instill fear or doubt into the minds of parents and teachers to create subservience to the reform.

This little gem comes from one toolkit:

"As changes take place, public resistance will increase unless a consistent encouraging message is echoed. For those messages to STICK, they must be repeated frequently and powerfully, and must be tied to other initiatives. People will remember and respond to the CCSS if the initiative is fresh in their minds and if they understand why this undertaking is critical for improved student outcomes. A successful CCSS communications strategy involves connecting with internal and external parts, engaging multiple audiences by building an effective coalition, and monitoring whether messages have been received and retained."

Sounds like something from *Mein Kampf*, if you ask me. I particularly like how the word "stick" is capitalized for emphasis. The condescending tone and implied brainwashing of the masses significantly underestimates the rising tsunami of parents that oppose this initiative intelligently, without constantly repeating the same words and phrases. The Educrats supporting this monstrosity certainly do *repeat* themselves a great deal.

In the following pages, I'll examine the most common messages they use. You can then judge their validity for yourself.

MESSAGE #1: THE CHILDREN BELONG TO ALL OF US

The message of collectivism is used to garner acceptance of a one-size-fits-all, centralized planning approach and make parents feel as though they need not concern themselves with education. One of my favorites is a Melissa Harris-Perry propaganda message from MSNBC, Microsoft's™ news station, that aired during a PGA golf tournament in 2013. In this public service announcement, available on youtube.com, Harris-Perry tells us:

We have never invested as much in public education as we should have. We haven't had a very collective notion of "these are our children." We have to break through our private idea that children belong to their parents, or children belong to their families, and recognize that children belong to whole communities. Once it's everybody's responsibility and not just the household's, we start making better investments.

Months later, Paul Reville, the former secretary of education for Massachusetts, said, "the children belong to all of us" at a panel discussion at the Center for American Progress (CAP) when discussing Common Core opposition. The CAP is an organization founded by George Soros (AIR test consortium). Oh, by the way, they got a half million dollars from Gates to promote Common Core.

This argument is not new. Since the 1920s, American parents have battled the state for authority over their children. Now we have the U.N. influencing policymakers as well with the Right of the Child. In the 1970s, Kurt Waldheim, Secretary-General of the U.N., addressed the Executive Board of UNICEF saying, "Until fairly recently, in most societies, the responsibility for child development rested entirely with parents.... This... is changing... The process of child development has to be the concern of society as a whole on the national and international level. From the very beginning, the leaders of UNICEF... clearly understood this...."[114] That vision found its way into state laws in the 1980s. In the 1990s, Hillary Clinton created a stir with "It Takes a Village."

This collectivist preaching devalues the individual and the family. Collectivism does not work in America. That is not what we stand for. America is about faith, family and individual freedom. Either these CCSS advocates truly believe in collectivism as part of their worldview, or they are simply regurgitating propaganda from across the pond, or both. If my kids really belong to all of us, then where the heck is everyone else when the baby pukes at 2 a.m.? I could use a little help!

Besides, the claim about not spending enough is hogwash to taxpayers. With the exception of the Reagan years, we have continually increased federal spending, up to 375% since 1970. And we spend more than most other countries too. Despite throwing money at this "problem," we are not seeing any return on our investment as test scores flat line. Darn facts.

MESSAGE #2: WE ARE LOSING TO CHINA

Another scare tactic is to make parents feel like our kids don't measure up to the whiz kids in Asia, particularly China. Nicholas Madison, Superintendent of the Brillion district in Wisconsin recently remarked at an assembly hearing, "[American} exceptionalism has come and gone with all due respect, Representative." Madison continued, "We have to be willing to innovate faster than the Chinese can copy us or our industry is going to go away. You talk about what country standards did you look at, here's what country I look at when I go down to Home Depot and see snow blowers made in China. That's a real problem...That is who we are competing with."[115]

Pardon me, Mr. Common Core, I know the Chamber of Commerce probably told you to say that, but the reason we have Chinese snow blowers has more to do with a trade agreement in 1999 (thanks, Bill Clinton) than education standards.

Professor Christopher Tienken wrote a great article about this called, "What PISA Says About PISA" and I highly recommend it. For 40 years, we've been told our kids are not testing well. Now we have a new international testing source, PISA, which the propaganda spinners can ma-manipulate. What is rarely noted, and enormously significant, is that the U.S. reports the scores of our *entire demographic* to the Program for International Student Assessment (PISA). You'll see why this is critical information.

FACTORS SKEWING SCORES: POVERTY

The U.S. demographic is one of the most diverse in the world. Our aggregate scores reflect a mix of extreme poverty and affluence; whites, blacks and Hispanics; multiple faiths; rural, suburban and city dwellers. All these factors influence an individual's attitude toward education, discipline and access to resources. We have plenty of research that demonstrates that poverty (not curriculum or teachers) is the biggest barrier to education success. The U.S. is constantly trying to close the achievement gap for its students, usually by throwing money at it.

China, on the other hand, is not nearly as diverse culturally; however, they have reform programs in place to extend education to the poorer, more rural areas of the country. They also have a significant early intervention program that offers preschool starting at age one. But here is the clincher: their PISA scores for literacy and math came from one affluent city, Shanghai—not the entire country or the rural areas that have a very different educational experience. That would be like the U.S. reporting only the wealthiest section of Massachusetts. In fact, over 74% of China's population lives in rural, poverty-stricken areas.

PISA data has been analyzed to try to obtain a more "apples to apples" comparison of U.S. data to other countries, given the way those countries gather and compile their data.

In 2012, Martin Carnoy and Richard Rothstein of the Economic Policy Institute analyzed the 2009 PISA data and compared U.S. results by social class to three top performers— Canada, Finland and South Korea. They found that the relatively low ranking of U.S. students could be attributed in no small part to a disproportionate number of students from high-poverty schools among the test-takers. After adjusting the U.S. score to take into account social class composition and possible sampling flaws, Carnoy and Rothstein estimated that the United States placed *fourth* in reading and *10th* in math – up from 14th and 25th in the PISA ranking, respectively.[116] (Emphasis added.)

This analysis clearly shows how PISA data can be manipulated by propagandists to create a false impression of a crisis. PISA specifically acknowledges that the scores are representative of several factors, including poverty, life experience, and culture, all factors that are difficult to accurately measure. Education reform is not limited to standards, testing, curriculum or teacher pay.

FACTORS SKEWING SCORES: CULTURAL DIFFERENCES

There are significant cultural differences between China and the U.S. that we should consider when we start comparing test results, including the stability of the family unit, poverty, early intervention and student mindset.

The United States ranks #1 in divorce internationally against 34 other countries. This is four times that of China, which comes in at #17 today. This is after the divorce rate has risen in China for the last seven years. Why is this important? According to research, by age 17, 81% of

American children of divorce experience at least one year of poverty compared to children of married households at 22%. This definitely has a negative impact on their ability to learn.

Another cultural difference that has an impact on PISA scores is family size. Chinese families are restricted to having only one child by law. We have a multitude of research studies in the U.S. that validate higher birth order equating with greater academic achievement and potentially higher IQ. In the U.S., the average family includes two children per household.

Furthermore, Chinese households typically have 1-3 generations under one roof. In Chinese culture, a substantial emphasis is placed on the value of education and social class. Grandparents and parents teach their children to obey authority and school is their top priority.

I grew up with my grandparents in the same house, but this is a dying trend in the U.S. Modern American families often follow job opportunities across state lines, leaving grandparents far away, only seeing their grandkids during holidays or vacations, at best. Most students today do not have a multi-generational influence keeping them focused. This also affects their understanding of history and culture, as they lack personal stories to enrich their textbooks. In today's American society, school, especially the early-intervention kind, often serves as daycare for parents who depend on two incomes to survive.

FACTORS SKEWING SCORES: EARLY INTERVENTION
There are studies indicating that early intervention improves academic achievement gaps. Thus, both the U.S. and China have made strides in bringing children into government education earlier in life, especially in

high-risk (typically high-poverty) populations. Yet, despite the research and the attempts over the last 40 years, little long-term progress has been made to demonstrate that this is necessary or helpful.

China offers "Infant School" starting at age one with some early-intervention programs of the boarding model. In the U.S., preschool offerings vary by state. Many are government-funded and available only to those who meet poverty-line criteria. More and more, government education is creeping into the childhoods of children in both countries.

Factors Skewing Scores: High-Stakes Assessments

China has relied on a model of education that hinges on high-stakes assessment. All students are required to take a test that determines whether they get into college as well as their place in life. In China, the National College Entrance Exam (gaokao) is about more than getting into college. Virtually all government positions require a college degree. Passing the exam also grants a higher level of social class, including the ability to change residency from one province to another (a privilege denied to migrant workers, therefore excluding them from government position and influence). When students do well on this test, they are treated like celebrities, with television segments and the opportunity to publish books on how to succeed.

It turns out that, according to Chinese business leaders in shiny Shanghai, all graduates really know is how to pass a test. They can't think on their feet and they are not meeting the innovative demands of China's high-tech industries. China has created a bunch of worker-bees.

In addition, over a third of college graduates cannot find work in China. "There is currently a surplus of college graduates unable to find work in innovative but elite private firms or oversubscribed government agencies. Meanwhile, the Chinese service industry, the mainstay of the U.S. economy, remains tiny. Unlocking the potential of that industry is going to take a radical overhaul of how the Chinese think about education. China is in the midst of education reform as well and doing so to fuel economic goals of creating a workforce"[117]

Whoops! Sound familiar, America? China is now focusing its education reform on what America was doing, prior to No Child Left Behind.

The focus on high-stakes testing has driven China into education reform and compromised the mental health of its students. There has been a rise in legal actions to redress grievances and evidence of soaring stress levels among Chinese students. The suicide rate is increasing so much in China that in 2013, a university asked its students to sign a suicide waiver. "Amid growing competition for university places and rising graduate unemployment, suicide is now the leading cause of death for Chinese people aged between 15 and 34"[118]

SUMMARY

We are a free nation and China is a communist republic so we do not share the same values. We are diverse in culture and report a range of aggregate data. China reports only the affluent Shanghai, leaving out 74% of its population. China brings children into government at age one. In America, kindergarten is still optional in some states. If we are to learn anything from China, it is that they share the same barriers to education: poverty and increasing destruction of the family unit, too much high-stakes testing, disregard for the well-being of the student, and too much government interference.

The Common Core State Standards Initiative seeks to increase high-stakes testing for our students and drive workforce planning and management through career testing. It puts students in a box and increases national government influence and regulation in education. This did not work in China, regardless of what the PISA Math and Literacy scores say.

Enough about China already. They're communists. We're free. Apples to oranges.

MESSAGE #3: OUR KIDS MUST BE ABLE TO COMPETE IN THE 21ST CENTURY GLOBAL ECONOMY

As a parent, I am still waiting for Mr. or Ms. Common Core to explain to me what will be so different about this elusive "21st Century Global Economy." The Common Core Propaganda Parade talks about it as if it is some kind of new, unknown thing: an alien environment that parents cannot possibly prepare their children for without help.

Let's get real. America was founded on global economic competition. As working parents, *we are* the global economy. Many of us travel for work to other countries and sell our goods overseas. As managers, directors, and owners we know what to look for in solid employees.

Despite our "broken" education system, America remains a dominant force as the largest economy with the most scientific discoveries. Students come here from overseas to attend our Universities, our scholars are known worldwide and we lead the globe when it comes to innovation and entrepreneurship. According to Innovation and Entrepreneurship in the Global Innovation Index of 2013, America even beat Asia, making the top five. China and Japan didn't even make the top ten.

DOES THE COMMON CORE HELP?

Yong Zhao is the presidential chair and associate dean for global education at the University of Oregon's College of Education and is a fellow of the International Academy for Education. Notably, he previously served as director of the U.S.-China Center for Research on Educational Excellence at Michigan State University, and served as the executive director of the Confucius Institute/Institute for Chinese Teacher Education. Most would agree his credentials are impeccable and his opinions worth consideration.

In an effort to establish a global managed economy, Yong Zhao says we're exposing our children to the same standardized content and delivery methods as the rest of the world and testing and monitoring them with the same government-sanctioned or funded, sophisticated data systems. The implication, of course, is that all these schools will turn out the same type of product. Oops. Worker. Equipped with standardized skills and basic knowledge.

Zhao's research attempts to answer the question of what is needed in the "new" global economy, in the absence of a response from the CCSSI. He found that the jobs of the next generation remain something of an unknown but he makes the case that jobs requiring standardized skills and basic knowledge are moving toward automation. Further, any lower- to middle-level jobs that aren't automated are likely to be moved overseas to cheaper markets.

America has already felt the sting of seeing many of our job opportunities move to India or China. For global competitiveness, what American students need is to stand out, to be innovative and creative and to provide a level of expertise that cannot be outsourced to the cheapest market. Which brings us back to where we have always excelled—innovation and entrepreneurship.

WHAT WE REALLY NEED

Richard Florida, an American economist, echoes this in his best seller, *The Rise of the Creative Class*, where he says, "design, story, symphony, empathy, play, and meaning, will become more valuable."[119] Another economist, Philip Auerswald, makes a convincing case for the need of more entrepreneurs.

According to Zhao, Common Core standardized education only serves to assess the test-taking skills of our students, which are generally left-brained cognitive skills. Innovation, entrepreneurship and creativity are right-brained skills and these are the necessary tools to be competitive. Zhao argues that by forcing children to master the same skills around the globe, we are preventing them from developing the skills that would set us apart and he says, "The efforts to develop common curricula nationally and internationally are simply working to perfect an outdated paradigm. The outcomes are precisely the opposite of the talents we need for the new era."[120]

The restrictions that come with common standards and testing not only limit the innovative power of our students, they limit innovation in the classroom itself. One of the biggest advantages of true local control is that our schools become local laboratories. By asking every school to do things the same way, on the same schedule, we lose the ability to grow and learn from each other. With Common Core, every school will do the bare minimum, teaching only to the government tests. Bored and unmotivated teachers will be bogged down trying to meet mandates set by the state and the U.S. DOE and completing insurmountable amounts of paperwork.

This does not equate to developing innovation or creativity in the classroom, which in turn does not result in creative or innovative students. However, it does result in a generation of factory workers and middle managers who can't get jobs on their own soil—and a generation that purchases gadgets built in other countries.

MESSAGE #4: WE NEED COMMON (NATIONAL) STANDARDS BECAUSE WE MOVE SO MUCH

The people behind these standards won't use the term "National Curriculum" because they know that is illegal. They won't say "National Standards" because they know that's not popular. So they changed the wrapper and labeled their program "*Common* Standards" instead.

Regardless of how shiny the package is, according to the U.S. Census only 1.7% of the K-12 population crosses state lines in a given school year.[121] That is hardly a justifiable argument for national or common standards.

To be assured the propaganda gets lots of attention, the Bill and Melinda Gates Foundation paid the Military Education Coalition "to develop and execute an advocacy campaign in support of the implementation of Common Core State Standards (CCSS) in multiple states by leveraging the voices and actions of its network of military families and uniform leadership." He constantly pits the Common Core op-opposition against our soldiers and patriotic Americans, implying that we are not supporting our military families if we don't support Common Core.

The ironic thing is that here in Arkansas, I met a mother who is married to an active duty soldier stationed overseas. She said the consequences of Common Core were so horrific in their Department of Defense school that she left her husband to his duty and returned home to the U.S. so she could home school her daughters (it is illegal to home school in Germany where they were based, a remnant of old Nazi law). The Common Core actually split that family apart.

MESSAGE #5: THESE STANDARDS ARE RRRIGOROUS

If I hear the word rigorous one more time from a Common Core pusher, I just might lose it. I mean it. Rrreally.

Rigor is the latest buzzword in education and educators and policy makers all have their own definition. The problem is that even the CCSSI cannot define rigorous for us, so they should really stop repeating it. Gutting previous state standards into something that is described as "fewer and deeper, not an inch thick or a mile wide" does not sound like *increasing rigor* to me. From where this parent sits, constructivist math that takes two hours and 100 circles to complete and gutting literature into excerpts isn't what I would call *rrrigorous*.

MESSAGE #6: THESE STANDARDS ARE COLLEGE AND CAREER READY

As a parent, if a reformer tells me they are preparing my child for college, I think of a four-year, selective university. However, the CCSSI defines "college-ready" as preparing students for a 2- or 4-year non-selective school. The goal is to get all students to a community college. Our U.S. Secretary of Education, Arne Duncan, confirmed this in his 2010 speech to UNESCO, where he touted the administration's goal for America to have the highest college attainment rate in the world by 2020. There is nothing wrong with community college, but let's call a spade a spade.

REBRANDED REFORM

Robert H. Burke, a California Legislator in the late 1960s, wrote a comprehensive report on the education reform measures that were being pushed in his state back then. The report is dated 1971 and titled, *Education: From the Acquisition of Knowledge to Programmed, Conditioned Responses.*

He summarized it this way:

They were as parts in a puzzle—analyzed by themselves, each of these projects appeared to be either harmless or an expression of someone's "dream." When linked together with other "harmless" programs, they were no longer formless but could be seen as an entire package of plans outlining methods of implementation, organization structures (including flowcharts), computerization, use of behavioral profile catalogs, and goals and objectives determination.[122]

Sound familiar? That is an accurate description of the CCSSI: four separate pieces that when presented alone don't seem like a big deal (just standards) or too spooky to be realistic (the data mining) until you put them all together in a pretty Race to the Top Package with a $4.35 billion bow on top. Despite the marketing efforts to describe the tentacles of this reform as "next generation" or "21st Century," the reality is that this package is the exact same reform that has been pushed since the 1930s.

Arne Duncan said, "A generation ago, America did in fact lead the world in college attainment. But today among young adults, the U.S. is tied for ninth."[123] Bill Gates also confirms that "U.S. [graduation] rates have not improved for 40 years,"[124] and "Yet college completion rates in the U.S. have been flat since the 1970s." [125]

A generation ago, the United States Department of Education did not exist. The U.S. Department of Education was not established until 1979 and didn't get off the ground until 1980. It is younger than most of to-day's parents.

Seems to me things have gone downhill significantly since then. The common denominator here is the U.S. government.

What was the standard for education a generation ago? Perhaps the answer lies in our past. For "The Greatest Generation" there were three standards: Reading, Writing and Arithmetic, which got us more than college attainment. Those standards got us to the moon. They also got us computers, software, microwave ovens—the list goes on.

The reformers just keep rebranding it and waiting for the next generation to forget the discourse. For generations the reformers have been slowly boiling the country (remember that frog!) into believing they want national standards, national tests and workforce-steering driven by data collection.

America does not want this reform and never has. A recent poll (2014) conducted by Rasmussen found that only 23% of Americans believe the federal government should set education standards for schools. In other words, *America does not want national standards.* It also found that over half of Americans believe schools place too much emphasis on standardized testing. Only 24% believe student scores on standardized tests should be a major factor in determining how well a school is doing. *In other words, America does not want national testing or outcome-based education.*

When it comes to the Common Core specifically, the poll found that 47% of parents with children currently in school oppose Common Core, with 19% undecided. 54% think it is unlikely to improve student outcomes. 44% of all Americans believe Common Core will not improve student performance.[126]

Clearly, the reformers do not have buy-in from parents because we cannot be bought by Gates or the U.S. Chamber of Commerce. We believe what we see in our children, not the propaganda we're being fed.

The answer lies in our past, with the Greatest Generation that dominated the global economy, space exploration, innovation and college attainment. Give us *less:* less central planning, less testing and less fear mongering.

Chapter

13

Now that David Coleman, the co-lead author of the Common Core standards, has become president of the College Board, we can expect that the SAT will be aligned to the standards. No one will escape their reach, whether they attend public or private school.[127]
- Diane Ravitch

The Threat to Private Schools and Home Schools

This reform poses a significant threat to private and home-schoolers with regard to testing, data collection and aligned curriculum. Since the national tests (GED, ACT and SAT) are aligning, both private and home school students may find themselves at a disadvantage if they do not learn the abstract methods of the Common Core standards. Furthermore, they will likely be exposed to controversial "informational text" subject matter on the assessments. Staying out of the classroom does not protect them.

PRIVATE SCHOOLS

Some private schools have adopted the Common Core State Standards, while others have "adapted," meaning they've taken bits and pieces from more than one set of standards to create their own. In this way, private schools may have incorporated all or some of these standards. The only way to know is to ask your private school.

This issue is creating a huge stir in Catholic dioceses right now. Over half of the Catholic dioceses have adopted or adapted Common Core standards. Why? Accountability and money, of course. First, the private schools need their students to outperform the public schools on standardized tests. When the tests are aligned to Common Core methodologies, the private school students could be at a disadvantage if they have not been taught according to those standards.

To help further this adjustment, the Bill and Melinda Gates Foundation gave a $100,000 grant to the National Catholic Educational Association (NCEA) "to support trainings and provision of follow-up materials for teachers on implementing the Common Core State Standards."[128] The NCEA then put together an initiative called the Common Core Catholic Identity Initiative to "provide resources to design and direct the implementation of Common Core within the culture and context of a Catholic school curriculum. Thus Catholic schools can infuse the standards with the faith, principles, values and social justice themes inherent in the mission of a Catholic school."[129]

To be fair, $100k is peanuts when it comes to money from the Bill and Melinda Gates Foundation. However, Gates has also given over $64 million in grants for other Catholic initiatives, including money to Catholic Relief Services and several specific projects in the state of Washing-Washington. It is reasonable to assume that there is some sense of "if you scratch my back, I'll scratch yours" between Gates and the Catholic Diocese.

Over 130 Catholic professors are not happy with Common Core, despite the fact that the propaganda machine says higher education just loves it. Last year they signed an open letter launched by Notre Dame Law Professor Gerard Bradley. They sent the letter to the all the U.S. bishops asking them to drop the standards, calling them "a grave disservice to Catholic education."[130] Parent advocacy groups for Catholic schools have also erupted, making the argument that if the private school is doing the same thing as a public school, why pay so much more for a private school?

At the U.S. Conference of Catholic Bishops, the Catholic education secretary responded politically by passing the buck to the local bishops, saying, "parents possess the fundamental right to choose the formative tools that support their convictions and fulfill their duty as the first educators."[131] That sounds more like an incentive to home school than to remain in a Catholic school. According to Ann Hynds, of Pittsburgh Catholics Against Common Core, I am not alone in that sentiment, "A *lot* of Catholic moms are seriously talking about home schooling and have already pulled their kids out of Catholic school."[132]

Private schools also determine their own testing sources, unless there are state laws that stipulate otherwise. One unexpected consequence occurred in Indiana under their voucher system. Before the state passed a voucher program, private schools could use various tests such as the

Stanford Achievement or the Iowa Test of Basic Skills. The voucher program stipulated that the private schools had to use the state test, which was replaced by the PARCC Assessment upon implementation of Common Core. Fortunately, Indiana has since repealed Common Core and withdrawn from the PARCC consortium.

HOME SCHOOLS

The Home School Legal Defense Association provides excellent research and advice on the effect of Common Core on home schools and I highly recommend that home school parents review it. It can be found at http://www.hslda.org/commoncore/topic7.aspx. They have also produced a documentary on Common Core called *Building the Machine*. It is available online, at no charge, at www.commoncoremovie.com and they are releasing more videos this year.

As states move away from existing testing contracts and into the Common Core consortiums, home schools may be pulled into PARCC or SBAC testing, depending on their state regulations for home school testing. This also presents a privacy data risk for home school students as the scores and other student information go into the State Longitudinal Data System (SLDS).

The federal mandates of the data collection initiative motivate states to consider including students outside its parameters. At the National Conference on Student Assessment in 2011 (yes, there is a national conference for testing), Oklahoma explained to the CCSSO how the challenge of meeting the data requirements of federal and state education policies are motivating them to "include student groups not now included (*e.g.*, home-schooled) in the data system."

FINDING COMMON CORE ALTERNATIVE MATERIALS

For generations, some families have chosen home school as a means of avoiding indoctrination and revisionist history. They now find it difficult to purchase materials not poisoned by the Common Core. Fortunately, a database has been created to help parents make good curriculum and testing decisions.

Headed by Tina Hollenbeck, a veteran home school teacher and member of the Educational Freedom Coalition, The Home School Resource Roadmap provides home school teachers with information they can use before purchasing virtually any home school resource under the sun. Tina personally spent countless hours calling and emailing each publisher and test developer to ascertain whether the materials are explicitly aligned or correlated to the Common Core. Home school teachers can decide to adopt Common Core or avoid Common Core by using this tool for research: http://www.hsroadmap.org/common-core-project/.

SHARED THREATS

The aligned curriculum poses the most obvious threat to both private and home schools. Even in the state of Texas, which did not adopt the CCSSI (they were duped by Common Core's evil twin brother, CSCOPE, which has also been repealed) parents and teachers are frustrated by the infiltration of Common Core materials in their schools.

To meet demand and keep their heads above water financially, most education publications have aligned their materials to the CCSSI. Now our books have decorative seals on the cover to indicate they've been hijacked by the risky reform. It's a brilliant marketing tool for those who like CCSSI or are forced to teach it.

For private schools, this becomes burdensome. The CCSSI-aligned math books use constructivist abstract methods that make parents feel they're wasting tuition money. The history and social studies books are full of indoctrination and revisionist history.

The important question arises yet again for private and home schools—where are they taking us? Over time, will these schools be dragged into this abyss with testing and data? Home school teachers in particular may be in for another round of protecting their rights to educational freedom (as was seen in the 1990s) and must remain vigilant.

Chapter

14

*Law and liberty cannot rationally become the objects of our love, unless
they first become the objects of our knowledge.*
- James Wilson, Of the Study of the Law in the United States, Circa 1790

Know Your Rights

SUPREME COURT RULINGS

While the Center for American Progress and MSNBC would like to
think that children belong to all of us (the State), the Supreme Court has
ruled differently. Parental rights are broadly protected by Supreme Court
decisions. In several cases, the Supreme Court held, on the basis of the
14th amendment, that while the State has a valid role in providing an
opportunity for every child to receive an education, it cannot override the
parents' primary duty to direct that education.

THE PARENT HOLDS THE RIGHT TO DIRECT THE CHILD'S EDUCATION, NOT THE STATE

In *Pierce v. The Society of Sisters* (1925), the Court said that "the child is not the mere creature of the State: those who nurture him and direct his destiny have the right coupled with the high duty to recognize and prepare him for additional obligations."[133]

In *Meyer v. Nebraska* (1923), the Supreme Court criticized the state for interfering "with the power of the parents to control the education of their own." [134]

In *Prince v. Massachusetts* (1944), the Supreme Court concluded, "It is cardinal with us that the custody, care and nurture of the child reside first in the parents, whose primary function and freedom include preparation for the obligations the State can neither supply nor hinder." [135]

The *Washington v. Glucksburg* case (1997) establishes that, "In a long line of cases, we have held that, in addition to the specific freedoms protected by the Bill of Rights, the 'liberty' specially protected by the Due Process Clause includes the rights . . . to direct the education and upbringing of one's children." [136]

FEDERAL LAWS

The Fourteenth Amendment "forbids the government to infringe... 'fundamental' liberty interests of all, no matter what process is provided, unless the infringement is narrowly tailored to serve a compelling state interest."

YOU HAVE THE RIGHT TO REFUSE SURVEYS AND SHARING OF PERSONAL INFORMATION

The Protection of Pupil Rights Act ("PPRA") of 1978, permits parents to inspect classroom materials and requires parental consent before psychiatric or psychological testing or treatment can be administered to students. The hitch is that it only applies to programs that receive funding from the U.S. Department of Education, so this may not apply if you have a student in a private school.

STATE LAWS

Several states have recently passed "opt-out" statutes that protect a parent's right to shield their child from objectionable content found in sex or health education courses, including New York, New Jersey and California to name a few.

The *Protection of Pupil Rights Amendment (PPRA)* of 1978, commonly known as the *Hatch Amendment* protects students and parents from U.S. Department of Education-funded programs that ask for students to complete surveys, analyses or evaluations that reveal personal information such as: psychological information, political affiliations, attitudes about sex, behaviors, religion, etc. There are several sample *Hatch Amendment* "Opt Out" letters available on the Internet, or you can craft one on your own. Either way, it is obvious that the Educrats have tried these data collection and utopian social change initiatives in the past and now we have laws protecting us from them.

Recently, additional state laws have included an "opt out" provision from standardized testing and data collection. Examples include Utah and Oklahoma. Coalition parents like me will say that we're refusing the tests, not asking permission to opt out. If you would like more information on how to refuse a test in your state, including a "Get Tough Guide," visit www.unitedoptout.com. Boycott the Common Core assessments and make your voice heard.

Other state laws of interest include laws regarding school choice, vouchers and home school. These issues vary by state. Examination of the laws in your state will empower you to make informed decisions about your child's education. I encourage all parents to look into the home school laws of their state. Private school may also an option. There has been much discussion in recent years about school choice and voucher systems. If these programs are allowed to proceed through our state legislatures, they will give parents who otherwise could not afford private school the opportunity for their tax dollars, almost $7,000 per year in most states, to follow their children into a private school or a virtual (online, computer based) home school. You can also vote with your feet. Walk your children right out of public schools.

On a personal note, private school is not a financial reality for me. If someone asked me a few years ago if I would consider home school, I would have laughed and said no way. I would have said I was not qualified to educate my kids. I would have said that I could not bear the thought of being home with them all day. Surprise. I withdrew my children from public school last year to home school them, and ate my words.

We *love* it. We are not hermits. We play sports. We are closer. It has been a most rewarding journey. I will continue to home school at least until Common Core is repealed in my state.

According to Eric Zimmerman of Regent University, "Advocates of a so-called 'Children's Rights' doctrine have questioned whether the law should still consider parents to be the best child-rearers. Although they speak of the rights of children, these scholars actually seek to transfer child-rearing authority from parents to the State by allowing judges, social workers, or other public officials to decide the type of education that children should receive."[137]

My child belongs to me. It is not the job of the State to clothe, feed, shelter or discipline my child. It is not the job of the State to provide healthcare to my child. It is not the job of the state to love my child. It is not the job of the state to educate my child. This is a free nation and as the parent I and I alone am responsible for MY CHILD. If I choose to hire the State to perform these tasks using my tax dollars (i.e. government school or government food or government healthcare) then that is my choice. If I want or need the help of the government to raise my child I will ask for it. Otherwise, the Constitution and Supreme Court law dictates that I am responsible for my child, Thankfully, here in *America*, the country that values family and freedom, we have the 14th Amendment to protect us from greedy social change agents. We just have to stop taking orders and invoke it. What we allow is what will continue.

NoChoiceNoVoice.com

Chapter
15

Rally Call

"It does not take a majority to prevail...
but rather an irate, tireless minority,
keen on setting brushfires of freedom in the minds of men."
~ Samuel Adams

WHAT COMMON CORE HAS ACCOMPLISHED

This reform was developed from a corporate perspective, taking workforce skills and backtracking them all the way to kindergarten. It is cognitively inappropriate, especially for young students in the concrete operational development stage, generally up to age 12. Instead of being challenged, they are being trained and sorted. These standards are hurting our children emotionally, breaking their spirits and attempting to mold them into a collective of subservient, citizen worker-bees.

Our children, who were once enthusiastic about school and performed well, are now coming home from school emotionally damaged. They're saying things like, "I hate school. I'll never get this. I'm not good at math. Do I have to go back? I'm so bored."

Mental health experts tell us they are seeing an increased number of kids due to depression and anxiety resulting from these education reforms. Parents report that their honor roll kids are being placed on academic improvement plans or are being sent to summer school because of a test score.

The proponents of Common Core will say that this initiative is rigorous and college-ready; that it prepares our kids for a 21st century global economy and encourages them to think critically. The reality is that their brand of rigor is not something we want in our public school classrooms because it is based on demanding, rank and file policy and procedures. It is only college-ready in the sense that it prepares students to take introductory classes at a 2-year, non-selective college, not a 4-year selective university. It teaches abstract constructivist, collectivist thinking, not critical thinking.

COMMON CORE ASSESSMENTS: OUR CHILDREN'S FUTURE

The standards aren't even the worst part. Common Core is an initiative, more than standards. In addition to shabby, unpatriotic standards that are cognitively inappropriate and clearly dumbing our children down, the initiative includes new high-stakes tests that have never been through pilot programs. Those tests are written by the same people pushing the standards and occur more often throughout the year with results tied to teacher performance evaluations. The initiative includes an excessive amount of data collection and sharing with the federal government and hundreds of other agencies.

Our children are now mandated by law to sit for career profile exams designed to feed them into workforce pathways before graduation. Their performance on the new assessments will dictate the classes they're allowed to take in high school, placing them on a career track in middle school, far younger than most of us were when we decided what we wanted to do for a living. The federal government, specifically the Department of Labor, is using private corporations and non-profit education agencies to lead us into a managed economy with increased centralized planning, tracking student responses to these tests in a database that provides no privacy protections.

All of this—the standards, the data collection, the work force pathways, the controversial supporting curriculum—are part of the Common Core State Standards Initiative. Two signatures unleashed this monster on our children on behalf of the state. (Remember, it only required the signatures of the governor and the appointed state school commissioner to put all this into effect.) It is a violation of our 10th, 4th and 14th Amendment rights, and three federal laws.

The Common Core State Standards Initiative fractures the parent-child bond, censors our beloved teachers, abuses our children and sets the stage for federal overreach beyond measure. It closes the door to our children's freedom and parental rights in the name of control and profit.

LIGHT THOSE FIRES

As an American mother, I am all for diversity and world-mindedness but I'm not giving up individualism, nationalism and state sovereignty in exchange for Common Core: a UN model of education focused on behavior change that uses unproven public-private partnerships. It is time to put education back in the hands of the parents, the teachers and the people. Our state legislatures need to regain control and throw this horrific reform into the dustbin of history forever.

ASSERT YOURSELF: GET OUT THERE AND GET CONNECTED

Parents cannot continue playing hooky when it comes to education. We've been trusting for way too long. You have to *show up*. It's not enough to click "Like" on Facebook or to rant about something on Twitter. It's not enough to simply email a legislator or a school board member. Parents have to make the time to *participate* in meetings—local school board meetings, PTO meetings, education committee meetings—any meeting where decisions will be made regarding your children's education. Parents need to get tough and teach the education system how to treat us. The system is funded by our tax dollars. It should work for us. Those buildings belong to us and we need to take our schools back. Instead of allowing social change agents and elitist CEOs to run our local school boards and drive them into the ground, parents need to get involved and start running for local school board positions.

Don't stop there. *Show up* at the capitol when your local coalition tries to push through a bill to protect your educational rights. Developing a personal relationship with your legislators and building credibility is key to overturning this reform in our states.

Apathy has given us the government we deserve. We can no longer be apathetic. We can no longer stick our heads in the sand and assume someone else will fight this battle for us. We can no longer use careers or social activities as an excuse for not getting involved.

We *must* get connected. We *must* be part of the solution. If not, then we will have the education system that we deserve, one that is run by multinational corporate elitists and a government that is too big, too nosey and doesn't have the best interest of your child at heart.

The movement against the Common Core is a national one. Each state affected by the CCSSI has a coalition and there are national networks formed to connect us. Over 30 states have legislation fighting back. Each coalition works to educate parents and legislators in our state and to bring legislation that protects the educational freedom of our children and the next generation.

This movement will go down in history as one that drew multiple generations, races, genders, political affiliations and individuals together for a greater cause, a *multi-partisan* movement that sets politics aside and places our children at the top of the priority list.

PARENTS MUST LEAD

The only real hope of establishing educational freedom in our country lies in grassroots efforts to reclaim local control. Parents must awaken to the idea that while other countries may disagree, education in America is about creating free minds and well-rounded individuals, not global change agents or human capital. Our founding fathers intended for families to be responsible for—to *own*—the process of educating their children, not the government or private corporations. The new education revolution must be parent-led.

The reformers have clearly underestimated the danger of crossing the line between a mother and her child. The reformers also have yet to learn the strength of the American family unit, family values, faith and individual responsibility. America was built upon these values and they cannot be destroyed easily.

Parents around the nation have awakened from their sleepy, apathetic state to take back the education of their children. Social media, community meetings, privately published books, citizen lobbying and organized protests are successfully bringing this initiative to its knees in true American Revolutionary form. While we may be late to the party, parents are not leaving until we reclaim our children as our own, along with their natural right to grow into free individuals, not human capital.

The 20th Century philosopher John Dewey said, "Education is not preparation for life. Education is life itself." Which begs the question, to whom am I giving my child's *LIFE*?

APPENDIX A:
Pearson Record of Incompetence

*Compiled by Bob Schaeffer, public education director of FairTest, a non-profit dedicated to ending the misuse of standardized tests.

1. 1998 **California** – test score delivery delayed.

2. 1999-2000 **Arizona** – 12,000 tests graded incorrectly due to flawed answer key

3. 2000 **Florida** – test score delivery delayed resulting in $4 million fine

4. 2000 **Minnesota** – mis-graded 45,739 graduation tests leads to lawsuit with $11 million settlement – judge found "years of quality control problems" and a "culture emphasizing profitability and cost-cutting."

5. 2000 **Washington** – 204,000 writing WASL exams rescored

6. 2002 **Florida** — dozens of school districts received no state grades for their 2002 scores because of a "programming error" at the DOE. One Montessori school never received scores because NCS Pearson claimed not to have received the tests.

7. 2005 **Michigan** — scores delayed and fines levied per contract

8. 2005 **Virginia** – computerized test mis-graded – five students awarded $5,000 scholarships

9. 2005-2006 **SAT college admissions test** – 4400 tests wrongly scored; $3 million settlement after lawsuit

10. 2008 **South Carolina** – "Scoring Error Delays School Report Cards" The State, November 14, 2008

11. 2008-2009 **Arkansas** — first graders forced to retake exam because real test used for practice

12. 2009-2010 **Wyoming** – Pearson's new computer adaptive PAWS flops; state declares company in "complete default of the contract;" $5.1 million fine accepted after negotiations but not pursued by state governor

13. 2010 **Florida** – test score delivery delayed by more than a month – nearly $15 million in fines imposed and paid.

14. 2010 **Minnesota** -- results from online science tests taken by 180,000 students delayed due to scoring error

15. 2011 **Florida** – some writing exams delivered to districts without cover sheets, revealing subject students would be asked to write about

16. 2011 **Florida** – new computerized algebra end-of-course exam delivery system crashes on first day of administration

17. 2011 **Oklahoma** – "data quality issues" cause "unacceptable" delay in score delivery ; Pearson ultimately replaced by CTB/McGraw Hill

18. 2011 **Guam** – score release delayed because results based on erroneous comparison data; government seeking reimbursement

19. 2011 **Iowa** – State Ethics and Campaign Finance Disclosure Board opens investigation of Iowa Education Department director Jason Glass for participating in all-expenses-paid trip to Brazil sponsored by Pearson Foundation

20. 2011 **New York** – Attorney General Eric Schneiderman subpoenas financial records from Pearson Education and Pearson Foundation concerning their sponsorship of global junkets for dozens of state education leaders

21. 2011 **Wyoming** – Board of Education replaces Pearson as state's test vendor after widespread technical problems with online exam

22. 2012 **New York** – "Pineapple and the Hare" nonsense test question removed from exams after bloggers demonstrate that it was previously administered in at least half a dozen other states

23. 2012 **New York** – More than two dozen additional errors found in New York State tests developed by Pearson

24. 2012 **Florida** – After percentage of fourth grades found "proficient" plunges from 81% to 27% in one year, state Board of Education emergency meeting "fixes" scores on FCAT Writing Test by changing definition of proficiency.

25. 2012 **Virginia** – Error on computerized 3rd and 6th grade SOL tests causes state to offer free retakes.

26. 2012 **New York** – Parents have their children boycott "field test" of new exam questions because of concerns about Pearson's process

27. 2012 **Oklahoma** – After major test delivery delays, state replaces Pearson as its testing contractor

28. 2012 **New York** – More than 7,000 New York City elementary and middle school students wrongly blocked from graduation by inaccurate "preliminary scores" on Pearson tests

29. 2012 **New York** – State officials warn Pearson about potential fines if tests have more errors

30. 2012 **Mississippi** – Pearson pays $623,000 for scoring error repeated over four years that blocked graduation for five students and wrongly lowered scores for 121 others

31. 2012 **Texas** – Pearson computer failure blocks thousands of students from taking state-mandated exam by displaying error message at log on

32. 2013 **New York** – Passage from Pearson test-prep book appears in Pearson-designed statewide test, giving unfair advantage to students who used those materials

33. 2013 **New York** – Pearson scoring error blocks 2,700 students from gifted-and-talented program eligibility

APPENDIX B:
Advice on Stopping the Common Core

1. Look for and find a parent-led coalition in your state at www.stopcommoncore.com.

2. Learn how to refuse the tests at www.unitedoptout.com.

3. Contact your state legislators and arrange to meet them in person. If you don't know who your legislator is, try this search engine: http://openstates.org/find_your_legislator/.

   • Do not threaten your vote and do not come across as angry.

   • A meeting in person goes further than an email. Build credibility and plant seeds of information over time. Refrain from unloading all at once.

   • Back up your concerns with documentation and share your personal story

4. Follow this web site to stay informed of our progress: www.truthinamericaneducation.com

5. If you use social media, follow this group on Facebook: Parents and Educators Against Common Core State Standards.

6. Run for your local school Board and join the PTO. Consider running for your state House or Senate.

7. Write a letter to the editor of your local newspaper.

APPENDIX C:
Recommended Reading and Viewing

Common Ground on Common Core: Voices from across the Political Spectrum Expose the Realities of the Common Core State Standards. Edited by Kirsten Lombard. Available at www.resoundingbooks.org

The Children of the Core by Kris Nielson

Uncommon by Kris Nielsen

The Deliberate Dumbing Down of America by Charlotte Iserbyt

Conform: Exposing the Truth About Common Core and Public Education by Glenn Beck

Common Core and the Truth (A Parent's Journey into the Heart of the Core) by Amy Skalicky

Watch this free documentary online:

Building the Machine at www.commoncoremovie.com

APPENDIX D:
Acronyms Used in this Book

ACT	ACT. (Originally "American College Testing") Standardized test used to measure high school achievement. Used by college admissions departments.
AFT	American Federation of Teachers. Trade union representing workers in education, health care and public service.
AIR	American Institutes of Research.
ALEC	American Legislative Exchange Council.
ARDOE	Arkansas Department of Education
ARRA	American Recovery and Reinvestment Act of 2009. Known as the Stimulus Act
BBE	Bully Bandwagon of Educrats.
CAP	Center for American Progress. Organization founded by George Soros. Received funding from Bill and Melinda Gates Foundation to promote Common Core.
CCSS/ CCSSI	Common Core State Standards/ Common Core State Standards Initiative.
CCSSO	Council of Chief State School Officers. D.C.-based group for state school officers
CEDS	Common Education Data Standards. One of two templates available for states to use in creating their longitudinal data systems.
CEO	Chief Executive Officer. Head of a corporation.
CSCOPE	A K-12 educational curriculum support system that has been widely adopted in Texas. It was created by the Texas Education Service Center Curriculum Collaborative (TESCCC).
ED	Abbreviation for the United States Department of Education
EIMAC	Education Information Management Advisory Consortium.
ELA	English Language Arts. The part of the Common

	Core including formerly traditional "literature."
EMO	Education Management Organization. For-profit organizations that run charter schools.
EPIC	Electronic Privacy Information Center.
FERPA	Family Education Right to Privacy Act.
GAO	Government Accountability Office, a non-partisan organization that works for Congress to investigate how tax dollars are spent.
ITBS	Iowa Tests of Basic Skills. Standardized test for K-8 in wide use before Common Core.
K-12	Grades Kindergarten through 12.
MOU	Memorandum of Understanding. Agreement between a state and one of the Consortiums (PARCC or SBAC) providing standardized testing/assessment tools.
NAEP	National Assessment of Education Progress.
NAGB	National Assessment Governing Board. Board governing mega-tests.
NCLB	No Child Left Behind. Education reform initiative passed by the George W. Bush administration.
NCTM	National Council of Teachers of Mathematics.
NEA	National Education Association. Labor union representing teachers, secretaries and educational support personnel.
NEDM	The National Education Data Model. One of two templates available for states to use in creating their longitudinal data systems.
NGA	National Governor's Association. Bipartisan organization of the nation's governors.
OECD	Organization for Economic Cooperation and Development. A group of 30 member countries that discusses and develops economic and social policy.
P-20	Data system model for State Longitudinal Data Systems to track students individually from Pre-K to age 20.

PARCC	Partnership for the Readiness of College and Careers. A Common Core test consortium.
PISA	Program for International Student Assessment. Test administered every three years by the OECD.
PPRA	Protection of Pupil Rights Act (1978). Permits parental inspection of classroom materials. Requires parental consent for psychological or psychiatric testing. Applies to programs funded by U.S. DOE.
RttT	Race to the Top. Initiative under Obama administration awarding federal funding to states that demonstrated willingness to adopt federal reforms.
SAT	Scholastic Aptitude Test. Standardized test used to measure high school achievement. Used by college admissions departments.
SBAC	Smarter Balanced Assessment Consortium.
SFSF	State Fiscal Stabilization Funds.
SLDS	State Longitudinal Data System.
TPA	Teacher Performance Assessment. Testing tool for teacher evaluation offered by Pearson Education.
U.S.DOE	United States Department of Education.
UNESCO	United Nations Educational, Scientific and Cultural Organization.
UNICEF	United Nations Children's Fund.
NCEE	National Center for Education and the Economy. Organization presided over by Marc Tucker.

About The Author

Karen Lamoreaux, author of *No Choice, No Voice: Something is Rotten to the Core*, is a married mother of three and a small-business owner in Maumelle, Arkansas. A board member of *Arkansas Against Common Core*, Karen's video-recorded opposition to the controversial reform package delivered to the Arkansas State Board of Education went viral on the Internet. Since then, Karen has been given a voice on *Fox and Friends*, the *Willis Report* on *Fox Business*, the *Glenn Beck Show*, the *Pat & Stu* radio show as well as local television and radio networks around the nation.

Together with her fellow coalition members, she travels statewide and regionally, educating other parents and legislators about the realities of Common Core and working toward its repeal by the Arkansas State Legislature. She advocates for the preservation of parental rights as well as state rights in education. She recently started homeschooling her children.

BIBLIOGRAPHY

http://eagnews.org/mississippi-superintendent-threatens-the-jobs-of-teachers-who-oppose-common-core/

http://missourieducationwatchdog.com/missouri-budget-amendment-8-for-tinfoil-hats/

http://truthinamericaneducation.com/common-core-state-standards/barbarians-at-the-gate-press-on-in-arizona/

http://www.eagleforum.org/educate/marc_tucker/

http://blog.heartland.org/2014/06/the-danger-of-big-data-and-the-progressive-plot-for-education/

http://news.heartland.org/newspaper-article/2013/04/24/state-led-common-core-pushed-federally-funded-nonprofit

http://www.nga.org/cms/about

http://news.heartland.org/newspaper-article/2013/01/03/tax-sponsored-common-core

http://www.ccsso.org/Documents/2011/Principles%20and%20Proc esses%20for%20State%20Leadership%20on%20Next-Generation%20Accountability%20Systems%20(Final)%20(2).pdf

http://www.ccsso.org/Who_We_Are/Business_and_Industry_Partn erships/Corporate_Partners.html

http://www.nga.org/cms/home/news-room/news-releases/page_2009/col2-content/main-content-list/title_common-core-state-standards-development-work-group-and-feedback-group-announced.html

http://deutsch29.wordpress.com/2014/06/22/common-core-mou-not-just-for-development/

http://www.washingtonpost.com/blogs/answer-sheet/wp/2014/03/11/teachers-union-cites-common-core-in-decision-to-cut-gates-funding/

http://www.globalinnovationindex.org/content.aspx?page=press-release

http://www.pearsoned.com/pearson-and-americas-choice-announce-acquisition-agreement/#.U6IoH_ldUpg

http://www.theguardian.com/education/2012/jul/16/pearson-multinational-influence-education-poliy

http://www.ecs-commoncore.org/aligning-early-childhood-education-with-the-common-core/

http://www.onenewsnow.com/education/2013/07/24/publisher-agrees-to-alter-controversial-passage-in-history-book#.U54myPldUph

http://freedomoutpost.com/2013/07/floridians-outraged-over-islamic-bias-and-indoctrination-in-school-textbooks/#2htCWGuVYUS7Z7bk.99

http://www.salon.com/2013/12/16/keep_fox_news_out_of_the_cla ssroom_rupert_murdoch_common_core_and_the_dangerous_rise_ of_for_profit_public_education/

http://www.theguardian.com/uk-news/2014/jun/24/scotland-yard-want-interview-rupert-murdoch-phone-hacking

http://www.washingtonpost.com/blogs/answer-sheet/wp/2013/02/09/global-education-market-reaches-4-4-trillion-and-is-growing/

http://wisconsindailyindependent.com/disturbing-testimony-at-hearing-reveals-what-is-at-the-core-of-common-core-support/

http://www.hslda.org/commoncore/timeline.aspx

http://www2.ed.gov/programs/statestabilization/guidance.pdf

http://www.washingtonpost.com/politics/how-bill-gates-pulled-off-the-swift-common-core-revolution/2014/06/07/a830e32e-ec34-11e3-9f5c-9075d5508f0a_story.html

http://www.corestandards.org/assets/CCSSI_ELA%20Standards.pdf

www.corestandards.org/assets/Appendix_B.pdfhttp://www.uaedreform.org/sandra-stotsky/

Mark Bauerlein and Sandra Stotsky. (September 2012). How Common Core's ELA standards place college readiness at risk. Pioneer Institute White Paper #89. http://pioneerinstitute.org/download/how-common-cores-ela-standards-place-college-readiness-at-risk/

R. James Milgram and Sandra Stotsky (September 2013). Lowering the Bar: How Common Core Math Fails to Prepare High School Students for STEM, Pioneer Institute White Paper #103. http://pioneerinstitute.org/news/lowering-the-bar-how-common-core-math-fails-to-prepare-students-for-stem/

http://www.act.org/commoncore/pdf/CommonCoreAlignment.pdf. http://www.act.org/epas/

http://www.publiceddread.com/2013/04/constructivism-reformed-into-common-core.html

http://media.collegeboard.com/digitalServices/pdf/research/10b_2901_Comm_Core_Report_Complete_WEB_101117.pdf

http://www.educationnation.com/index.cfm?objectid=D8F266A4-0693-11E2-BC7C000C296BA163

http://frizzleblog.scholastic.com/post/kellogg-foundation-announces-new-investment-%E2%80%98family-and-community-engagement%E2%80%99

http://www.ed.gov/edblogs/technology/files/2013/02/OET-Draft-Grit-Report-2-17-13.pdf

http://www.ed.gov/edblogs/technology/research/

http://heartland.org/policy-documents/research-commentary-arkansas-common-core

http://www.corestandards.org/assets/CCSSI_Mathematics_Appendix_A.pdf

http://www.newhavenindependent.org/index.php/archives/entry/gates_chips_in_1m/

http://blog.heritage.org/2013/09/22/common-core-lacks-common-business-sense/

http://jaypgreene.com/2013/03/21/constructive-criticism-for-common-core-constructivism-deniers/

http://www.breitbart.com/Big-Government/2013/12/13/Exxon-Mobil-CEO-Strongly-Encourages-Pennsylvania-Governor-to-Implement-Common-Core

http://truthinamericaneducation.com/common-core-state-standards/kids-who-move-across-state-lines/

http://www.achieve.org/files/CCSSandFocalPoints.pdf

http://www.huffingtonpost.com/jed-applerouth/deconstructing-the-new-sa_b_5206926.html

http://www.futurereadyproject.org/communications-planning

CAP Children belong to all of us:
http://m.youtube.com/watch?v=N3qtpdSQox0

http://www.breitbart.com/Big-Government/2014/02/03/Center-For-American-Progress-Panelist-On-Common-Core-The-Children-Belong-To-All-Of-Us

http://www.cato.org/publications/congressional-testimony/impact-federal-involvement-americas-classrooms

http://www.washingtonpost.com/blogs/answer-sheet/wp/2013/01/08/five-key-questions-about-the-common-core-standards/

http://truthinamericaneducation.com/common-core-assessments/indiana-private-schools-and-parcc-assessments/

http://www.foxnews.com/politics/2014/04/15/catholic-classrooms-face-common-core-overhaul/

http://www.cardinalnewmansociety.org/CatholicEducationDaily/DetailsPage/tabid/102/ArticleID/3280/U-S-Bishops-Acknowledge-Common-Core-Concerns-Affirm-Importance-of-Catholic-Mission-in-Schools.aspx

http://www.washingtonpost.com/blogs/answer-sheet/wp/2013/12/02/catholics-split-over-common-core-standards/

http://www.breitbart.com/Big-Government/2014/01/24/Catholic-School-Parents-Organize-To-Oppose-Common-Core-Standards

http://truthinamericaneducation.com/common-core-state-standards/support-for-common-core-plummets-with-parents-of-school-aged-kids/

http://www.crisismagazine.com/2013/common-core-goes-global

http://www.eagleforum.org/educate/2006/june06/moscow.html

http://teacher.scholastic.com/products/scholasticprofessional/authors/pdfs/duke_sample_pages.pdf

http://www.parentalrights.org/index.asp?SEC=%7B3051ABFF-B614-46E4-A2FB-0561A425335A%7D

http://aclj.org/education/parental-rights-in-education

NOTES

[1] http://eagnews.org/mississippi-superintendent-threatens-the-jobs-of-teachers-who-oppose-common-core/

[2] http://www.arkansased.org/state-board

[3] http://www.eagleforum.org/educate/marc_tucker/

[4] http://www.crossroad.to/articles2/05/ed-watch/12-2-unesco-gates.htm

[5] http://blog.heartland.org/2014/06/the-danger-of-big-data-and-the-progressive-plot-for-education/

[6] http://www.benzinga.com/media/cnbc/14/02/43435 59/craig-barrett-wants-stricter-u-s-k-12-education-standards

[7] http://truthinamericaneducation.com/common-core-state-standards/an-implied-threat-to-remove-exxon-mobil-from-states-that-refuse-common-core/

[8] http://www.nga.org/cms/about

[9] http://news.heartland.org/newspaper-article/2013/04/24/state-led-common-core-pushed-federally-funded-nonprofit

[10] http://news.heartland.org/newspaper-article/2013/01/03/tax-sponsored-common-core

[11] http://www.ccsso.org/Who_We_Are/Business_and_Industry_Partnerships/Corporate_Partners.html

12 http://truthinamericaneducation.com/common-core-state-standards/david-coleman-2-years-ago-we-were-a-collection-of-unqualified-people/

13 http://theline.edublogs.org/2011/11/02/common-core-director-to-you-no-one-gives-a-st-what-you-think-or-feel/

14 http://achieve.org/P-20-data-systems

15 http://news.heartland.org/newspaper-article/2013/01/03/tax-sponsored-common-core-meetings-closed-public

16 http://www.nga.org/cms/home/news-room/news-releases/page_2009/col2-content/main-content-list/title_common-core-state-standards-development-work-group-and-feedback-group-announced.html

17 http://www.gatesfoundation.org/media-center/speeches/2009/07/bill-gates-national-conference-of-state-legislatures-ncsl

18 http://www.washingtonpost.com/blogs/answer-sheet/wp/2014/03/11/teachers-union-cites-common-core-in-decision-to-cut-gates-funding/

19 http://www.crisismagazine.com/2013/common-core-goes-global

20 http://www.unesco.org/new/en/education/themes/leading-the-international-agenda/education-for-all/partners/public-private/

21 http://miamiherald.typepad.com/nakedpolitics/2014/03/from-common-core-to-immigration-jeb-bush-shows-hes-the-eat-your-broccoli-republican.html

[22] http://miamiherald.typepad.com/nakedpolitics/2014/
03/from-common-core-to-immigration-jeb-bush-shows-hes-the-
eat-your-broccoli-republican.html

[23] http://whatiscommoncore.wordpress.com/2013/03/23
/top-ten-scariest-people-in-education-reform-7-sir-michael-
barber-cea-pearson/

[24] http://www.pearsoned.com/pearson-and-americas-choice-
announce-acquisition-agreement/#.U6IoH_IdUpg

[25] http://www.theguardian.com/media/2011/mar/01/
pearson-libyan-investment-authority-stake

[26] http://www.phschool.com/about_pearson/

[27] http://www.wbir.com/story/news/local/2013/12/02/
parental-complaints-over-tn-textbooks-set-stage-for-
debate/3801721/

[28] http://www.onenewsnow.com/education/2013/07/24
/publisher-agrees-to-alter-controversial-passage-in-history-
book#.U54myPldUph

[29] http://www.onenewsnow.com/education/2013/07/24
/publisher-agrees-to-alter-controversial-passage-in-history-
book#.U54myPldUph

[30] http://freedomoutpost.com/2013/07/floridians-outraged-over-
islamic-bias-and-indoctrination-in-school-
textbooks/#2htCWGuVYUS7Z7bk.99

[31] http://www.foxnews.com/us/2013/11/10/common-core-
lessons-blasted-for-sneaking-politics-into-elementary-classrooms/

[32] http://www.theguardian.com/education/2012/jul/16/
pearson-multinational-influence-education-poliy

[33] http://www.washingtonpost.com/local/education/
pearson-pays-77-million-in-common-core-
settlement/2013/12/13/77515bba-6423-11e3-aa81-
e1dab1360323_story.html

[34] http://www.washingtonpost.com/blogs/answer-
sheet/wp/2014/05/06/a-history-of-pearsons-testing-problems-
worldwide/
[35]

http://www.salon.com/2013/12/16/keep_fox_news_out_of_the_
classroom_rupert_murdoch_common_core_and_the_dangerous_
rise_of_for_profit_public_education/

[36] http://www.theguardian.com/uk-news/2014/jun/24/scotland-
yard-want-interview-rupert-murdoch-phone-hacking

[37] http://www.washingtonpost.com/blogs/answer-
sheet/wp/2013/02/09/global-education-market-reaches-4-4-
trillion-and-is-growing/

[38] http://wisconsindailyindependent.com/disturbing-testimony-
at-hearing-reveals-what-is-at-the-core-of-common-core-support/

[39] http://heinemann.com/shared/onlineresources%5CE02123%
5CNewkirk_Speaking_Back_to_the_Common_Core.pdf

[40] https://www.youtube.com/watch?v=DuO_nB7WY9w

[41] http://www2.ed.gov/news/staff/bios/duncan.html

[42] http://www.washingtonpost.com/blogs/answer-sheet/wp/2013/11/16/arne-duncan-white-surburban-moms-upset-that-common-core-shows-their-kids-arent-brilliant/

[43] http://truthinamericaneducation.com/common-core-state-standards/luetkemeyer-addresses-common-core-concerns-to-arne-duncan/

[44] http://www.eagleforum.org/educate/2006/june06/moscow.html

[45] http://unesdoc.unesco.org/images/0015/001502/150262e.pdf

[46] http://unesdoc.unesco.org/images/0005/000569/0569 26eo.pdf

[47] http://unesco.usmission.gov/duncan-forum.html

[48] http://nces.ed.gov/programs/slds/stateinfo.asp and http://nces.ed.gov/programs/slds/faq_grant_program.asp#recov ery

[49] http://www2.ed.gov/news/pressreleases/2009/06/ 06082009.html

[50] *http://www.hslda.org/commoncore/timeline.aspx*
[51] http://www2.ed.gov/programs/statestabilization/ guidance.pdf

[52] http://www2.ed.gov/news/pressreleases/2009/06/ 06082009.html

[53] http://www.ecs-commoncore.org/aligning-early-childhood-education-with-the-common-core/

[54] http://www.washingtonpost.com/politics/how-bill-gates-pulled-off-the-swift-common-core-revolution/2014/06/07/a830e32e-ec34-11e3-9f5c-9075d5508f0a_story.html

[55] https://www.youtube.com/watch?v=AApeR8VyxCl&feature=youtube

[56] http://pioneerinstitute.org/blog/blog-education/blog-common-core/common-core-was-neither-internationally-benchmarked-nor-state-led/

[57] www.corestandards.org/assets/Appendix_B.pdf

[58] http://teacher.scholastic.com/products/scholastic professional/authors/pdfs/duke_sample_pages.pdf

[59] http://www.edweek.org/ew/articles/2011/12/14/14 wilson.h31.html

[60] http://www.schoolsmatter.info/2012/04/david-colemans-global-revenge-and.html

[61] http://books.google.com/books?id=b7Y-1c0DC6IC&pg=PA3&lpg=PA3&dq=Mark+Turner,+%22Narrative+imagining%E2%80%94story%E2%80%94is+the+fundamental+instrument&source=bl&ots=ebriBgdiTS&sig=z5DmG_v6t_TXyVA vuANrNHRcqwY&hl=en&sa=X&ei=l6LUU-z6EMWqyASO8ICoCA &ved=0CD8Q6AEwBA#v=onepage&q=Mark%20Turner%2C%20%2 2Narrative%20imagining%E2%80%94story%E2%80%94is%20the% 20fundamental%20instrument&f=false

[62] http://www.breitbart.com/Big-Government/2013/09/12/Arizona-School-District-Pulls-Sexually-Explicit-Book-Recommended-by-Common-Core-Standards

[63] http://www.politichicks.tv/column/warning-graphic-common-core-approved-child-pornography/

[64] http://www.freerepublic.com/focus/news/3090039/posts

[65] https://www.youtube.com/watch?v=xCoOv_DwaAk

[66] http://www.breitbart.com/Big-Government/2014/01/14/Expert-Dr-Sandra-Stotsky-On-Common-Core-We-Are-A-Very-Naive-People

[67] http://whatiscommoncore.wordpress.com/2013/09/07/notre-dame-conference-address-of-dr-sandra-stotsky-common-cores-invalid-validation-committee/

[68] http://www.cga.ct.gov/2014/EDdata/Tmy/2014HB-05078-R000312-Sandra%20Stotsky-TMY.PDF

[69] http://www.corestandards.org/assets/CCSSI_Mathematics_Appendix_A.pdf

[70] R. James Milgram and Sandra Stotsky. Lowering the Bar: How Common Core Math Fails to Prepare High School Students for STEM. (September 2013).

[71] http://connect.freedomworks.org/news/view/435322?destination=news

[72] http://connect.freedomworks.org/news/view/435322?destination=news

[73] What the United States Can Learn from Signapore's World-Class Mathematics System. http://www.air.org/sites/default/files/downloads/report/Singapore_Report_Bookmark_Version1_0.pdf

[74] http://unesdoc.unesco.org/images/0015/001502/150262e.pdf

[75] http://www2.ed.gov/about/bdscomm/list/mathpanel/report/final-report.pdf

[76] http://www.gse.harvard.edu/news-impact/2013/01/do-the-math/

[77] http://jaypgreene.com/2013/03/21/constructive-criticism-for-common-core-constructivism-deniers/

[78] http://www.publiceddread.com/2013/04/constructiv ism-reformed-into-common-core.html

[79] http://www.achieve.org/files/CCSSandFocalPoints.pdf

[80] http://www.washingtonpost.com/blogs/answer-sheet/wp/2013/01/29/a-tough-critique-of-common-core-on-early-childhood-education/

[81] http://whatiscommoncore.wordpress.com/2013/10/29/dr-gary-thompson-testifies-to-wisconsin-legislature-common-core-test-is-cognitive-child-abuse/

[82] *http://www.act.org/epas/*

[83] http://www.act.org/commoncore/pdf/CommonCore Alignment.pdf.

[84] http://media.collegeboard.com/digitalServices/pdf/research/10b_2901_Comm_Core_Report_Complete_WEB_101117.pdf

[85] http://www.huffingtonpost.com/jed-applerouth/deconstructing-the-new-sa_b_5206926.html

[86] http://nces.ed.gov/programs/youthindicators/index.asp?ShowFileName=Introduction.asp

[87] www.ed.gov/edblogs/technology/files/2012/03/edm-la-brief.pdf

[88] http://www.ccsso.org/What_We_Do/Education_Data_and_Information_Systems.html

[89] http://forumfyi.org/files/DQCbrief_Mar19_FINAL.pdf

[90] http://nces.ed.gov/programs/slds/faq_grant_program.asp

[91] http://nces.ed.gov/programs/slds/edci.asp

[92] http://nces.ed.gov/programs/slds/edci.asp

[93] http://whatiscommoncore.wordpress.com/2013/03/20/white-house-hosts-datapalooza-built-on-common-core-tests/

[94] https://www2.ed.gov/programs/racetothetop-assessment/parcc-cooperative-agreement.pdf

[95] https://www2.ed.gov/programs/racetothetop-assessment/parcc-cooperative-agreement.pdf
[96] https://www2.ed.gov/legislation/FedRegister/finrule/2008-4/120908a.html

[97] http://www.alec.org/model-legislation/student-data-accessibility-transparency-accountability-act/.

[98] https://www2.ed.gov/legislation/FedRegister/finrule/2008-4/120908a.html

[99] http://www.identimetrics.net/education_solutions.asp

[100] http://www.resistinc.org/newsletters/articles/parents-organize-ban-scan

[101] http://pippaking.blogspot.com/2007/05/kim-cameron-microsoft-has-been-blogging.html

[102] http://www.nap.edu/openbook.php?record_id=12720&page=1

[103] http://epic.org/2010/09/national-academies-releases-ne.html

[104] http://edlibertywatch.org/2013/08/feds-resolute-yet-tone-deaf-on-data-collection-part-1/

[105] http://www.washingtonpost.com/blogs/answer-sheet/wp/2014/03/14/netflixs-reed-hastings-has-a-big-idea-kill-elected-school-boards/

[106] http://nces.ed.gov/programs/coe/indicator_cgb.asp

[107] http://www.advancementproject.org/news/entry/civil-rights-education-justice-groups-file-title-vi-complaints-in-chicago-n

[108] http://www.washingtonpost.com/local/education/eight-groups-apply-to-open-new-dc-charter-schools/2014/03/11/62c37b08-a92c-11e3-8599-ce7295b6851c_story.html

[109] http://www.kansascity.com/news/local/article339572/In-a-jab-at-Common-Core-opponents-Missouri-House-panel-recommends-8-for-tin-foil-hats.html

[110] http://truthinamericaneducation.com/common-core-state-standards/barbarians-at-the-gate-press-on-in-arizona/

[111] http://www.arizonadailyindependent.com/2014/06/30/az-dept-of-education-to-anti-common-core-teacher-what-a-fcktard/

[112] http://truthinamericaneducation.com/common-core-state-standards/with-huppenthals-loss-in-az-school-chief-race-that-makes-barbarians-3-educrats-0/

113

http://www.edweek.org/ew/articles/2013/08/21/02pdk_ep.h33.html

[114] http://www.crossroad.to/text/articles/whtpr96.html

[115] http://wisconsindailyindependent.com/disturbing-testimony-at-hearing-reveals-what-is-at-the-core-of-common-core-support/

[116] http://neatoday.org/2013/12/03/what-do-the-2012-pisa-scores-tell-us-about-u-s-schools/. 07/12/2014.

[117] http://www.thesolutionsjournal.com/node/1077

[118] http://www.rfa.org/english/news/china/suicide-09112013114030.html

[119] http://www.washingtonpost.com/blogs/answer-sheet/wp/2013/01/08/five-key-questions-about-the-common-core-standards/

[120] http://www.washingtonpost.com/blogs/answer-sheet/wp/2013/01/08/five-key-questions-about-the-common-core-standards/

[121] http://truthinamericaneducation.com/common-core-state-standards/kids-who-move-across-state-lines/

[122] http://www.hourofthetime.com/1-LF/Hour_Of_The_Time_08142012-Education_Programmed_Conditioned_Responses-Robert_Burke.pdf

[123] http://www.ed.gov/news/speeches/vision-education-reform-united-states-secretary-arne-duncans-remarks-united-nations-ed

[124] http://www.gatesfoundation.org/media-center/speeches/2009/07/bill-gates-national-conference-of-state-legislatures-ncsl

[125] http://www.gatesfoundation.org/media-center/speeches/2009/07/bill-gates-national-conference-of-state-legislatures-ncsl

[126] http://www.rasmussenreports.com/public_content/lifestyle/education/39_think_common_core_standards_likely_to_improve_student_achievement

[127] http://www.washingtonpost.com/blogs/answer-sheet/wp/2013/02/26/why-i-oppose-common-core-standards-ravitch/

[128] http://www.gatesfoundation.org/How-We-Work/Quick-Links/Grants-Database/Grants/2013/09/OPP1097200

[129] https://www.ncea.org/sites/default/files/documents/ncea_commoncorestatestandards_053113.pdf

[130] http://www.washingtonpost.com/blogs/answer-sheet/wp/2013/11/02/catholic-scholars-blast-common-core-in-letter-to-u-s-bishops/

131

http://www.cardinalnewmansociety.org/CatholicEducationDaily/
DetailsPage/tabid/102/ArticleID/3280/U-S-Bishops-Acknowledge-
Common-Core-Concerns-Affirm-Importance-of-Catholic-Mission-
in-Schools.aspx

[132] http://www.breitbart.com/Big-
Government/2014/01/24/Catholic-School-Parents-Organize-To-
Oppose-Common-Core-Standards

[133] http://www.parentalrights.org/index.asp?SEC=%7B3051ABFF-
B614-46E4-A2FB-0561A425335A%7D

[134] http://www.parentalrights.org/index.asp?SEC=%7B3051ABFF-
B614-46E4-A2FB-0561A425335A%7D

[135] http://www.parentalrights.org/index.asp?SEC=%7B3051ABFF-
B614-46E4-A2FB-0561A425335A%7D

[136] http://www.parentalrights.org/index.asp?SEC=%7B3051ABFF-
B614-46E4-A2FB-0561A425335A%7D

137

http://www.regent.edu/acad/schlaw/student_life/studentorgs/la
wreview/docs/issues/v17n2/Zimmerman.pdf

Made in the USA
Lexington, KY
25 April 2015